"I'm glad you wrote the book."

-Parren J. Mitchell
Member of Congress

"Life in a Baltimore cab ain't always pretty."

-Dan Rodricks
Action News & Baltimore Sun Papers Columnist

"Good book . . . Maybe all of us represent these faceless characters at one particular time."

-Kweisi Mfume
WEAA Radio/City Councilman

"Fascinating material . . . Men and women open up and tell you the most personal things like they would tell a psychiatrist."

-Elane Stein
WBAL Radio

"Too few people believe in themselves, cab driving author observes."

-E. Lee Lassiter
News American Columnist

"There's nothing more real than the streets."

-Alan Christian
WFBR Radio

"Probably no one has a better feeling of the way people think than the cabbie."

-Joe Lombardo
WBAL Radio

"Taxi driver tells of encounters on the low road. He has seen more in his career as a cab driver than before as a cop."

-Anita Lewis
News American Staff

HEY CABBIE

HEY CABBIE

Written by
Thaddeus Logan

Edited by
Marion Bonaparte
Professor, Community College of Baltimore

Jack Dawson
Feature writer, The Baltimore Sunpapers

Lucy J. Miller
Educator, Baltimore City

LE.
Logan Enterprises Publishing Company
Baltimore, Maryland

Hey Cabbie, Fourth Edition, by Thaddeus Logan. Published 2012

Copyright © 1983 by Thaddeus Logan
Reprints: 2012, 1986, 1985, 1984

All rights reserved. No part of this book may be reproduced, stored in a retrieval system, or transcribed, in any form or by any means, electronic, mechanical, photocopying, recording, or otherwise, without the prior written permission of the publisher: Logan Enterprises Publishing Company, Post Office Box 23465, Baltimore, Maryland 21203.

Library of Congress Catalog Card Number 84-90417 Printed in the United States of America
Fourth Edition

  ISBN-13: 978-1477621370
  ISBN-10: 1477621377

Photograph of author: Gwendolyn Bruce
Cover: Downtown Scene (Howard at Lexington) Baltimore, Maryland

IN GRATITUDE...

To the memory of my father, Thaddeus Sr. and Uncle William (Box) Harris

To my mother, Bernice Butler

To my children, Jonathan & Monica

To Gwen for support, along with others

and

Khalil T. Adolemaiu-Bey

Author's Note

These writings feature a Baltimore cabbie, his fares and the city he serves. They are **genuine human interest stories** that will keep you intrigued. It shows a side of Baltimore rarely seen by most and gives a **view of human nature** as seen through the eyes of a perceptive cabbie. It demonstrates how the forces of positive thinking and attitude work in the industry. The bright and dark sides of Baltimore are seen through descriptive vignettes which allow the reader to re-live the cabbie's experience which portray that **PEOPLE ARE PEOPLE** no matter who they are or where they reside. Many of their problems stem from **SEX, POWER, MONEY, DRUGS** and **ROCK & ROLL**! This is any large city USA or the World dealing with the Haves/Have Nots or Rich Man/Poor Man.

Logan, a seasoned cab driver, recounts his experiences as a Baltimore City driver.

T. L.

www.HeyCabbie.net

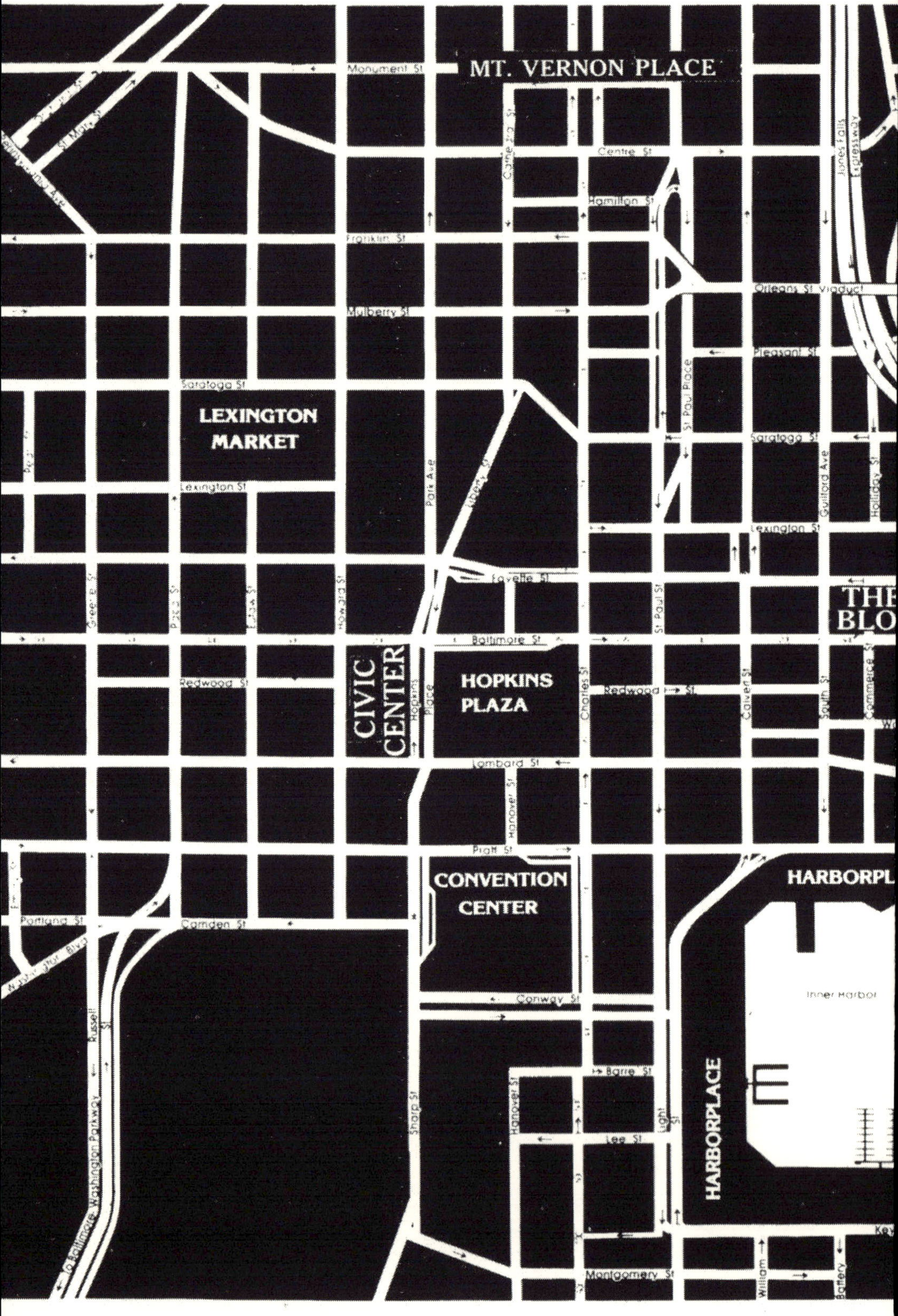
MT. VERNON PLACE
LEXINGTON MARKET
CIVIC CENTER
HOPKINS PLAZA
CONVENTION CENTER
HARBORPLACE
Inner Harbor
Monument St
Centre St
Hamilton St
Franklin St
Mulberry St
Orleans St Viaduct
Pleasant St
Saratoga St
Lexington St
Fayette St
Baltimore St
Redwood St
Lombard St
Pratt St
Camden St
Portland St
Conway St
Barre St
Lee St
Montgomery St
St Mary St
Cathedral St
Park Ave
Liberty St
Howard St
Eutaw St
Paca St
Greene St
Hopkins Place
St Paul Place
St Paul St
Charles St
Hanover St
Calvert St
Guilford Ave
Holliday St
South St
Commerce St
Jones Falls Expressway
Light St
Sharp St
Russell St
Washington Blvd
To Baltimore Washington Parkway
William
Battery

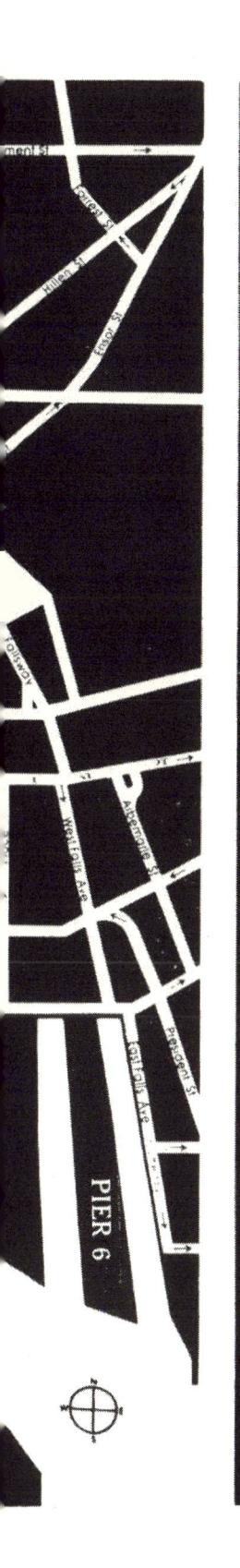

BALTIMORE CENTER CITY

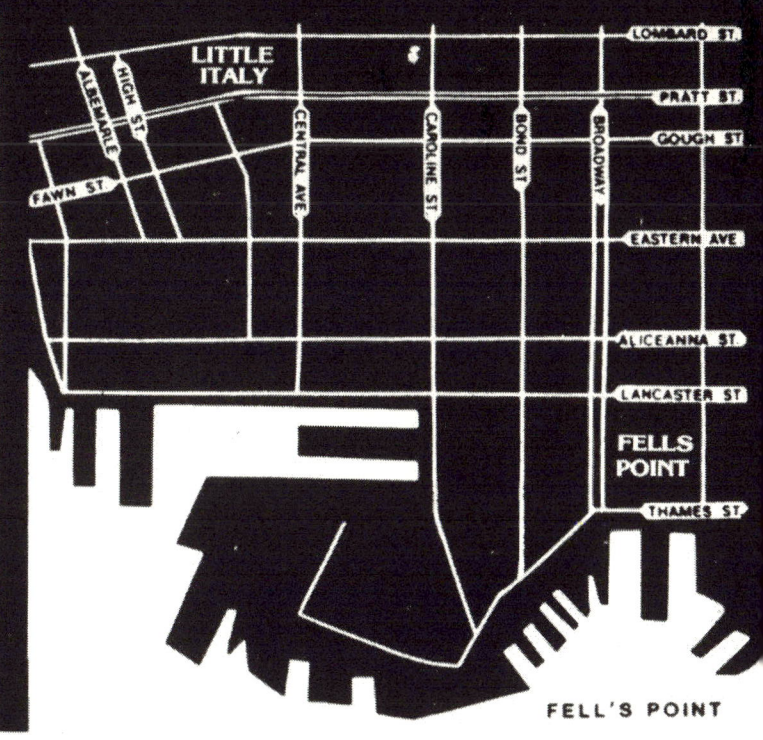

HEY CABBIE

NO ONE IN LIFE KNOWS WHAT THE FUTURE HOLDS. This was my last job for the evening, and I'd informed my friend that I'd be over about 11 p.m. It was pouring rain and the James Cleveland Gospel Show had just ended at the Civic Center.

Four soaked ladies flagged me at Baltimore and Howard Streets. After they were seated, they said that they wanted to go to three different locations. The first was the 2000 block of Bentalou Street. En route, one lady commented to another, "What a night to be out!"

They talked about how they had been touched by the James Cleveland Show. I asked if there had been a capacity crowd, and one of them said the Civic Center was about seventy-five percent filled.

I was traveling north on Fulton Avenue and decided to duck the traffic lights on North Avenue by making a left turn onto Westwood Avenue. At the intersection of Westwood and Appleton, a car ran the stop sign, hitting the taxi on the left front fender, causing me to lose control of it, and for it to veer off sideways in a perpendicular direction.

From the force of the impact, the lady sitting up front was knocked to the right door then back toward me as the taxi skidded to a stop. The lady's head hit my head like a rock, knocking my tooth through my lip. She became hysterical and hollered, "Oh, Jesus what's happening?"

The car that hit us careened to the left, hitting a parked vehicle. The man put his car in reverse and backed off the parked car. He got out of his vehicle, walked around to the taxi, looked me dead in the face and heard the ladies screaming. The man hurriedly got back into his vehicle, turned his lights off, backed his car up to Payson Street and left the scene.

I had learned when I was a policeman to try not to panic in such situations. When I had noticed the man walking fast toward his car, I could read his mind! So I focused in on the tag number and wrote it down. I asked my passengers if anyone was hurt and if an ambulance was needed. The lady up front was bent over and kept saying, "Oh, Jesus."

I attempted to use the taxi's radio but it was shot! It had apparently been knocked out in the collision. A resident offered the use of his telephone. I called the taxi company and advised them to send the police and an ambulance. I also said that I needed a tow truck for the taxi. When the ambulance arrived, the lady who was hollering, "Oh, Jesus," refused to be taken to the hospital.

Everyone else in the taxi said that they were all right. When the cop arrived on the scene, I gave him the description of the man and the tag number. He wanted to know how I had the presence of mind to take the tag number down and I replied that I had been a policeman for eight years and sensed the man was going to leave the scene.

While giving the cop the information, I asked him if my lip was cut badly. He looked into my mouth with his flashlight and said it was torn and that I could use a stitch or two. He took me to Provident Hospital in his police car. When I was released from the hospital, I couldn't even get through for a taxi, so I started walking toward the garage. It was raining and I was becoming wet, cold and miserable.

En route, I hailed this Royal taxi on Liberty Heights Avenue. At the garage, I filled out the necessary papers and paid off what was owed for the shift. Then I left and stayed off for the next eight days. Not once in eight days did anyone call and ask how I was doing! I knew that I had a case so I just played the game.

Hey Cabbie

When I returned to work, I had to see the insurance safety man. He wanted to know how I was going to handle this and if I had built up additional medical expenses. I told him that I wanted a healthy cash settlement and that he could be my mediator. He told me that he would start working on this immediately and not to forget about him. After I told him what I wanted, my involvement in the case was settled within two weeks.

The personnel man wanted to see me, stating that I owed additional money stemming from the accident. For curiosity, I asked him what would have happened if I had not obtained the tag number. He said that I would have had to pay for the damages. "You must be kidding me!" I said. "Why would I have to pay when I had witnesses in my favor?" That changed his tone, but I felt like saying "forget this company!"

Regardless of anything else, the cab company never loses! At the trial I wasn't represented by anyone from the company. Although the man was found guilty from my expert testimony, I still think that the taxi company should have sent a lawyer to represent me. From this experience, I realize more and more every day that you are in this world alone...!

It all started during the spring of 1979. My life was in complete turmoil, with all relationships going downhill. My divorce was pending after three years. I had girlfriend problems. I worked at a sales job that I hated. About the only positive thing that took place was that I finally completed college after eight long grueling years of attending evenings. I needed a break! So I decided after graduating from the University of Maryland to quit my job, pay my bills in advance, and take a trip to the West Coast in my green two-seater Datsun 240-Z, something that I had desired to do all my life. Only this time my purpose was twofold. I wanted to fulfill a fantasy and to blow cobwebs from my brain.

California was one trip that I'll never forget. It was the best experience of my life! At the time, I was thirty-four. It was the first time in my life that I was actually out there all alone! There was no time for indecisiveness. Many times prompt decisions had to be made for my safety and survival. This experience really contributed to me becoming a man!

    I drove across Country on Interstate 70 West and returned on Interstate 40 East. The drive was exciting, invigorating, and just adventurous. The geographical features of this country are breathtaking. At times I thought that I was re-living my United States History courses. Once I reached Los Angeles, however, I was disappointed. The city resembled none that I had ever encountered. Its downtown was like any other large metropolitan city, but other sections appeared to be little villages in valleys off the freeways. The width of the city streets and the mile high palm trees was too much for me to comprehend. The city just had too much space. I'm used to the cities here in the East, with small curved streets, people going about their daily businesses, with the full protection of large buildings.

    However, I loved the laid back, casual atmosphere of the Californians! You are what you are or into, whatever. Like who really cares? In that respect California is definitely different! However, many of my friends from Baltimore seemed lonely there. Some had no friends and many just missed home. They were interested in "What's happening in Baltimore." They knew more gossip about the place than I did. Some were into illicit drugs and heavy love affairs. Unemployment was high and there were no jobs. Most of my friends had graduated from colleges years ago but were forced *to hustle for a living*. My friends either shared apartments or lived off someone. None of them had those extravagant homes or that ocean front property. It was beautiful and I felt liberated, but it was not for me. Most of my friends including myself appeared to be caught up in some crises in life. This led me to realize that you cannot run away from your problems!

    I talked to my children and family by telephone on various occasions and was actually beginning to miss them. I realized that air fare for two was quite expensive. I did not want to be a stranger to my children. So, with this in mind, along with other factors, like a shortage of **MONEY**, I left Los Angeles.

    I returned to Baltimore after two months of wandering around the country. While conditioning myself to settling back into the Baltimore environment, I asked myself, "What's next?" The first thought that came to my mind was to use my previous related work experiences and find a job. My efforts proved fruitless after six weeks of pounding the bricks. Mind you, this was 1979. Here I was a college graduate, an experienced industrial salesman, a former Baltimore City policeman and vice detective for eight years, a former postal employee, and I could not find a job. I kept hearing that either I was **under or over-qualified**. I could not even find a $10,000 a year job with all those qualifications. I can just imagine what people are going through today!

My money was getting low and I could not survive much longer without generating some type of income. I thought about pushing a hack, remembering how lucrative the business was while moonlighting when I was a cop. No matter how frustrating, humiliating, and embarrassing it would be, this was something that I had to do for my survival. Believe me, you name it, I've heard it! "Why am I doing this type of work for a living?" I would shut up all critics by simply by asking, "Do you have a job for me, or will you pay my rent and child support?" Anyway, I knew that if I hustled, I would be able to make my ends meet fairly well.

So I took a temporary job with a local cab company, anticipating a REAL job in the near future. Nothing ever developed after circulating hundreds of resumes and going on numerous interviews in the Baltimore/Washington Metropolitan area. I changed my clothes out of the trunk of the cab more than once for job interviews. Then I would find myself seated among a bunch of young people waiting my turn to be interviewed. Then, for the next two weeks or so, I would wait anxiously in anticipation of a favorable reply. Some replies offered a second interview, but that was the extent of it, so I started keeping the courtesy rejection letters of why they would not hire me. To date, I have a bundle! All I can say is that it's **really tough out there!**

After a year, I just gave up. I stopped mailing resumes and going on interviews. I gave the cab business my undivided attention and started enjoying my life style. I did not have to worry about being late for work or what I was going to wear on the job; plus I was making money listening and learning from people and at times giving them advice. These life stories became so intriguing that I started writing them.

One fare left the cab at Ten Light Street and another got into the taxi. He told me to take him to Cooks Lane and

Hey Cabbie

Edmondson Avenue. While driving, he revealed that he had a half load on and that was the reason why he decided to take a taxi home.

He also told me that he was a tug boat ship captain and that during World War II he was assigned to a submarine in the Pacific. I asked if he ever had experienced depth charges and was he ever scared down there?

He told me that you are naturally scared of dying, but that they were brainwashed and trained to accept the situation, figure out the best possible solution, don't panic, and attempt to solve the problem.

He stated that if your fear was evident to others that this would and could cause panic to every individual on the ship. I think what the man was saying was that one of the crew members would kill you if necessary, before allowing you or another crew member's fright to panic the entire ship. This man told me that this type of behavior should be practiced to some degree when dealing with whatever crisis that you may be involved in life. He added that many excellent swimmers drown because they panic, get cramps and go under.

I told the man that I understood, revealing that I was once employed as a Baltimore City policeman. At times I was scared, but I tried never to show my fear when involved in a crisis. He said that he was sure that crisis situations had occurred in my taxi, and if I had not maintained calmness it is quite possible that something dangerous could have happened. Before the man left the taxi, his final note was to always try to accept a crisis situation, figure out a solution, and try to the best of your ability to maintain calmness. I thought that this was excellent advice!

A cabbie's awareness of the city means a lot to patrons. They like to feel secure and to know that a cabbie knows the road. If nothing else, a cabbie should know the main arteries throughout the city and the most direct route between points "A" and "B." Cabbies should be aware of the major cultural and social events in the city such as Harbor Place, the Convention Center, Civic Center, theaters, concert halls, etc. Cabbies should carry Baltimore's promotional magazine, **Good Times**. People will also ask you directions and for good restaurants. They may ask about the history of buildings, landmarks, and monuments. They look at you as a "source" and appreciate being in the company of a knowledgeable cabbie.

Parked at the taxi stand on Pratt Street in front of Harbor Place. These four white dudes, who later said that they were merchant marines from England, instructed me to drive them to the Coal Piers in Curtis Bay. While driving they told me they enjoyed the Inner Harbor and what it offered. I told them the Inner Harbor has brought love and charm to this city and that Baltimoreans love it.

It presents a relaxing, casual, and seaport atmosphere. We have quaint shops, restaurants, and market places. On the north side of the harbor is the Aquarium and an observation deck on the top floor of the World Trade Center. The Science Center is located on the south side. We have an amphitheater for FREE outdoor performances located between the Harbor Place Pavilions. Sometimes the entertainers will ask you for a donation. There is always activity at the Harbor; strolling, munching, sipping, flirting, jogging, browsing and shopping!

On a hot, humid night, there is always a big crowd at the Harbor. During the summer weekends, the Inner Harbor's Rash Field and Hopkins Plaza host numerous ethnic festivals. At these festivals, they sell their cultural foods and wares. At times, they also have top notch entertainment.

A biggie during the winter is celebrating the last minutes of the old year on New Year's Eve with fireworks. The summer ends with the City Fair at the Harbor.

Baltimore is a black-white city, but strolling the Inner Harbor, one can see changes from the old days. Interracial couples are more and more prevalent. I think the Inner Harbor is like the South. There is the South, and then you have Florida, a tolerant state in the Deep South, surrounded by Georgia, Alabama, South Carolina and Mississippi. Florida presents a laid-back atmosphere for relaxing and leaving your problems elsewhere. The Inner

Hey Cabbie

Harbor in Baltimore appears to possess the same image. It seems that many people go there to unwind after a hard day at work or to relieve themselves of their frustrations. The irony of it all is that this ideal place is located right in the center of our city. To date, many, many Baltimoreans still have not visited the Inner Harbor. I don't know why.

Baltimore has a very strong mayor whose project was to redevelop the Harbor front area around Pratt Street, Light Street, and Key Highway. It took time, but the task was completed, bringing tourism to downtown Baltimore. I congratulate the mayor on a job well done. **Time Magazine** *ran a cover story on the developer of Harbor Place and an article on the Mayor of Baltimore. The national magazine did a terrific job promoting Harbor Place, the Inner Harbor, and the City of Baltimore. This publicity has helped our tourist trade. People are vacationing now in downtown Baltimore. The attractions have increased the city's tourist trade by twenty percent.*

As a cabbie, out-of-towners constantly stop and ask directions to the Inner Harbor. Not a day passes without an inquiry. The streets, parking garages and parking lots in the Inner Harbor area are always filled with out-of-town vehicles.

The Pratt Street Pavilion is one of the few places in downtown Baltimore that has a cab stand. Many good jobs come out of Harbor Place going as far away as Annapolis, Washington, D.C. and Virginia. The local work is also fairly decent. The weekend business is very good to and from the Harbor. Large yellow taxi directories have been installed in the vicinity of the Inner Harbor. When a patron wants a taxi, he or she presses a button to signal a cruising cabbie in the vicinity. The flashing light can be seen for quite a distance. Harbor Place of the Inner Harbor has aided the cab industry immensely.

The Hyatt Regency, which is part of a major hotel chain, has a five-hundred-unit building directly across from Harbor Place's Light Street Pavilion. The top floor of the hotel has a club that overlooks the Inner Harbor and the outer Harbor of Baltimore. The view at night is spectacular! The nearby Convention Center books large conventions and groups from all over the country. I've heard that the Convention Center has bookings well into the 1990's. The Inner Harbor and its accommodations are major selling points for Convention Center booking; all of these factors spell money for the taxi industry.

Real estate in the downtown area near the Inner Harbor has skyrocketed! The city-operated parking lots that will eventually be redeveloped into some-thing modern and commercial are priceless. I would guess that open land in the area costs a million dollars an acre.

The rehabilitated townhouses in the residential section of the Inner Harbor area, known as Otterbein Place, are selling for almost one-hundred thousand dollars. Several years ago, these houses were uninhabitable shells. People bought them for one dollar. Many of the white middle class that had moved to suburbia over the past three decades are returning to this urban area to buy these vacant and abandoned properties around the city. Once they renovate them they are required to live in them for two years. The appreciation of real property in the area makes it a sound investment.

Pier Six's Harbor Lights Music Festival has done much to draw large crowds to the downtown area. The concerts are held throughout the summer.

The North Shore of the Inner Harbor will soon host a Six Flags Amusement Park. It will be an **indoor timeless entertainment center** for everyone located on Pier 4 in the old Gas and Electric Power Plant. It's scheduled to open in the spring of 1985. Parking will definitely be a problem! Also some six national hotel chains are presently under construction in the vicinity of the Inner Harbor.

After giving my spiel on the merits of Baltimore, one dude interrupted to say, "Taxis are much cheaper here than in England." "Oh yeah, really?" I asked "Why?"

"I really don't know, blimey," the young man replied. "But I'll tell you this much, practically everyone in England

Hey Cabbie

uses the public mass transportation system because of it." He told me in his broad English dialect that a journey like this, from downtown to the coal piers, would run about sixteen dollars.

"Well," I said, "at tops, the fare won't be any more than seven dollars, but I will accept what you think it ought to be." They all got a laugh out of that. The fare came to six dollars and eighty five cents. They paid the fare, and because of my spiel on the City of Baltimore, my charm, friendliness and sense of humor, they gave me a substantial tip.

As they were leaving, one dude asked, "Can we book your services and the use of your taxi for 6:00 p.m.?"

"I am sorry, but you see it doesn't work that way in Baltimore," I replied. "When you desire a taxi, simply call the company, and they'll send you one." "It's different back in England, taxies can be booked weeks in advance," he said. You learn something new every day in this business.

Beyond the Inner Harbor, many tourists inquire about and admire the old Bromo Seltzer Tower and the old B & O Railway Station at the foot of Howard Street. They especially like the old architectural structure of the Bromo Tower. The Inner Harbor appears to be the new commercial center. Howard Street was once the retail garment shopping section of the city but a couple of major department stores have left. It appears that the city is attempting to revitalize the area by hanging banners on lamp poles, placing benches for bus patrons, and painting the words "BUS STOP" very large at these locations, just below the name of the Mayor of Baltimore City. Let's face it; Howard Street seems to have lost something over the years. Only time will tell what will become of Howard Street!! Within the not too distant future, Interstate 95 will be completed through the state of Maryland. A spur of Interstate 95 will be situated at the foot of Howard Street in the vicinity of the old B & 0 Railway Station and the Convention Center. This will enable motorists or vacationers to be right at Baltimore's Inner Harbor once they exit the interstate. Baltimore is alive and well as seen every day through the eyes of a perceptive cabbie.

It was late and I was becoming hungry. So I decided to eat at Pollack Johnny's on the "B<small>LOCK</small>", the red-light district. I noticed this cute light-skinned chick hugged up with two Vietnamese dudes while parking in front of the Two O'Clock Club. She asked if I was in service. I said, "Always doll," and thought to myself, "So much for that bite to eat." One of the dudes told me to take them to a street in the vicinity of York and Belvedere. While driving up Greenmount Avenue both men were feeling and kissing all over the woman. The dudes talked in their native tongue while attempting to fulfill their sexual desires.

"Are you for real?" I asked her. "You're going to screw these foreigners in a private setting while they talk that shit around you?" "Yeah, tell me about it," She replied softly, "You do what you have to do."

She told me that these "boat dudes" had some big paper and she'd make it worthwhile for me to wait. Within my heart, I just couldn't leave the woman in this predicament. She told me to give her twenty minutes. I didn't own a watch, so I turned the taxi meter on and waited for thirty jumps. The meter jumps one and a half times a minute when motionless. After the time had elapsed, I left the taxi and went up to the house. One of the boat dudes came down the steps dressed in his blue jeans, he peeped from behind the door curtain and asked who was there. I told him that I was the cab driver and that the lady told me to return for her. The hooker came halfway down the steps with only a pair of blue argyle tights on. She told him to let me in. She added that she'd be ready in a minute. The man showed me pictures of his family in Vietnam that he missed. The hooker took the other dude in the backroom. Moments later she re-appeared fully clothed and said, "Let's go."

In the cab, she counted the money like a shark, which was $90, gave me twenty dollars, and told me to take her to Broadway and Oliver. Broadway and Oliver and the immediate vicinity is known for drug trafficking. "I felt

*sorry for you and you turn out to be a **FUCKING JUNKIE**," I told her. Right then my attitude changed!*
*At Broadway and Oliver, the hooker or junkie got out of the cab and found some dude that was **HOLDING**. They walked around the corner as they made the **DEAL**. She inspected the package after she got into the cab. I told her that I'd never seen a person FIRE and asked if I could watch. I told her that I wanted to see her **mood change as she mellowed out**. She told me that she wouldn't mind, but she had a professional hit woman in the high rise 200 project building on Aisquith Street. Informing me that this woman CAN REALLY FIND THAT VEIN, she said, "I don't think the lady will fire me up with a visitor." At the 200 Aisquith Street building, I simply said, "Good night."*

Baltimore is located in the northeast corridor of the country, about forty-five miles north of Washington, D.C. in the state of Maryland. It is a seaport and industrial city, best described as a working class town. The city is one of the oldest in the country. The boundaries are fixed, streets are narrow, and people live close together. The only way that the city expands is to rebuild on existing land or to construct tall buildings. The city is presently going through a face-lifting process with emphasis placed on the Inner Harbor, downtown, commercial areas, revitalization of neighborhoods, and commercial shopsteading. The climate is unpredictable with humidity that can be uncomfortable. One never knows when it is going to rain. This region experiences all seasons with cold and sometimes snowy winters, and hot sweltering summers. There is an ethnic heritage which consists of many diverse neighborhoods.

The majority of residences are row-houses, initially built for blue-collar-workers. The uptown houses are detached and at one time housed only the elite. Some of the uptown neighborhoods appear to be almost suburban, but still within the city. The terrain is somewhat hilly. The streets are tree-lined and contain a lot of curves. Many of the streets are named after famous people or family names, i.e. Bonaparte. There are accessible interstate approaches from all directions to Baltimore. It is the largest city in Maryland.

Baltimore is the eleventh largest city in the country. Its population is approximately 800,000, a decline of over 100,000 since the 1970 census. Roughly 55 percent of the population is black. Although they are the majority group, blacks feel they are underrepresented in the city government. Blacks do hold some key positions in the city government and private industry, however.

Unemployment in this city is high! The poor basically live in a ring surrounding the downtown area which is also the oldest section of the city. This is where most of the projects and low income units are found. The needs of these people are the same as anyone else; food, shelter, and clothing. Some inner city dwellers depend on federal, state, and city agencies concerning their survival. This stems from lack of education, lack of awareness, and the unemployment situation. For some, drugs and the drug business is a way of life for them to cope and to survive. Some uptown neighborhoods have turned into "ghettos" partly due to the development of interstate roads and other construction in the inner city. People had to relocate somewhere!

Further out, one comes to the ethnic, older and more stabilized neighborhoods. As you advance from one ring to another, inner city or ghetto style living disappears. Next are the homeowners and moderate apartment sections of the city. These sections are much quieter, peaceful, and, at times, safer than the inner city neighborhoods. Other project units are located on isolated land tracts around the city, such as Cherry Hill, Hollander Ridge, and Freedomway. Most homeowners have cars and have little need for taxi services. It is a rarity for many to use a cab. Only some type of a crisis in their lives would make it necessary for them to call or hail a cab.

I bidded on this call at the Medical Arts Building located at Read and Cathedral Streets. These two elderly ladies about seventy years old approached the cab - one black and the other white. One gave me a name, and asked if I was there for them. I said, "Yes." The black lady was carrying some packages and assisted the white lady in the cab. The white lady asked to be transported to upper Charles Street. The ladies talked among themselves until they reached their destination. The black lady called the white lady "Miss whatever" and the white lady referred to the black woman by her first name.

At the apartment complex on Charles Street, the white lady paid the initial fare and instructed me to give the change to her **"GIRL".** I thought to myself "girl". They both looked like the blind leading the blind! As they exited the cab, the apartment doorman opened the cab door and was given a dollar for his services. My tip for chauffeuring was a quarter. That's heavy! It was very hard for me to understand this lady's logic.

* * *

I was cruising in the vicinity of Park Heights and Belvedere and bidded on a call at Sinai Hospital. A white hillbilly of about fifty years old entered the cab and asked if I had come for him. Even if I wasn't there for that particular person, I would not tell him to leave if he looked presentable. As a cabbie I am always there ready to serve people as long as they have those **BUCKS.** Anyway, the fare said that he wanted to go to a cheap motel in Pikesville. The man said he was tired and had been with his wife for the past sixteen hours. He said his wife was a heart patient and that she had to have a special pacemaker installed at the hospital. He said his wife was flown in on a hospital plane from Alabama and that he had to get here the best way he could. The man said he was poor! He started to drive, but his son encouraged him to fly. He told me he had borrowed four hundred dollars from a friend and his son had arranged a discount air fare through his employer for a round trip to Baltimore. Then he said, with his Southern hillbilly drawl, **"Boy where there is a will, there is a way for us poor folk. Somehow or another what has to be done gets done."**

I was about to make a right turn onto Park Heights Avenue from Northern Parkway. As I was driving north on Park Heights, the fare noticed this synagogue and asked me what it was. I told him it was a synagogue because the majority of the people in this neighborhood were Jews. He said, "Jews! If I was a Jew, I would not be having these

financial problems because Jews really stick together." He
*shared a situation at home concerning a Jew. His business
was destroyed by fire and the man had no insurance, "Do
you know that the Jew's friends put him back on his feet.*
THEY REALLY STICK TOGETHER!"
*He went on to talk about the difference in cultures and
customs with people between the North and South. He said
that Southerners have a high regard for **HONESTY** and feel
safe down there. They really don't have to live in extreme
fear of others or like prisoners in their homes. He went on
to say that his best friend was a colored person who used
to live in New Jersey. His friend told him that when he
owned a car in New Jersey, he wrapped a linked chain
around the steering wheel and brake at night. Also, he
padlocked the hood of the car.*
*I said, "That ain't too unusual around here. Unemployment
is high and people do steal. Some may steal for their
survival and others as a vice. At the fare's destination, the
meter read four dollars, plus twenty-five cents for the call.
He gave me a ten dollar bill, told me to keep the silver and
to give him a five dollar bill. After wishing the man the best
of luck, regarding his frankness and financial situation, I
felt like saying that the cab fare was on me!*

    A major frustration of cab driving is working when others are not - Saturdays, Sundays, holidays, and late hours into the evenings. That's because cabbies make money when the masses are off. It is costly for me to take off on Sunday or the day before a holiday, but sometimes you have to for your own peace of mind. Also, a cabbie has to work ten to twelve hours a day on the owner/lease system in order to make it. The owner/lease system means that the cabbie is an independent businessman in a sense, but has to pay rental and gas on the equipment. It can take anywhere from four to six hours before a cabbie sees a dime profit. Dealing with the public can be very frustrating, but once they have exited the cab, you never have to deal with them again in life! Most of my work is done on weekends.

    Cab driving is definitely a hustle, what you put in is what you get out. Need I say more? All one can make is a living, you will never get rich, but "Those who bullshit, go home with bullshit." To make money in the cab business, you have to have the right attitude, strong motivation, and no deviations from your work. It makes no difference who you work for; your main objective is to make "MONEY."

Sometimes you have to step on the toes of fellow hack operators under the same colors in order to go home with a profit. What I mean is that you literally take telephone work or street fares that were promised to other cabbies. "They all do it." That is why it is known as a cold, legitimate hustle from the beginning.

Once you get hustling in your system, it is very hard to shake. It is one of the few jobs that I know of where one can go to work with nothing and return after his shift on any given good day with a very good cash profit. You know that there is always money out there if you want it. Making that ready cash makes a big difference rather than waiting for a check every two weeks. I believe making money from cab driving can get into your system like "dope." It is tough to just walk away from!

I was cruising in the vicinity of Morgan State University and bidded on a call at York and Woodbourne in Govans. The process of cab bidding is when the cabbie is cruising in the general vicinity of a particular intersection that is dispatched over the cab radio. A case in point would be 33rd and Greenmount Streets. The cabbie will key the microphone and say, "999, 33rd and Greenmount." This is the number painted on the exterior and interior of the taxi. Then the dispatcher will say, "999 pick up Jones at the Boulevard Theater." The cabbie repeats the name and location and responds in search of the fare.

Now back to York and Woodbourne; I responded after receiving the exact location from the dispatcher. An elderly looking white gentleman peeked out the front door and signaled for me to come into his house. At that location I left the cab, went to the door, and discovered he was a cripple clothed only in his underwear. He told me to go around to Rosen's Liquor Store and purchase him a pint of "Knotty Head gin." He gave me a five dollar bill and instructed me to turn the meter on. When I returned with the "booze," the meter read two dollars fifty cents. He gave me four dollars and told me to keep the change. He then asked if I wanted a drink. I told him "No thank you."

Cab drivers are a mixed breed. They include the highly intelligent to the ignorant, those who live well to welfare recipients, high school dropouts to college graduates, sport fanatics and theater buffs, Americans and foreigners, blacks and whites, men and women, homosexuals and heterosexuals, drug dealers and drug users, part-timers and full-timers, and gamblers and religious fanatics. The diversity is phenomenal, but in this industry there seems to be no secrets about their behavior. Many may appear to be dropouts in life, judging from their dress and demeanor, but they are not in reality. **"Cabbies are not closet people."**

This black bespectacled woman hailed me at the intersection of Park and Baltimore. She appeared disgusted and asked if it was alright if she sat up front. I said, "Fine." After the lady got comfortable, she lit a cigarette, and started talking about her boyfriend who was a cabbie. She said that she wished he would get a nine to five job and give that cab shit up. She said that she would like to see him have stability and security in life. Presently, he only works when he needs money and most of the time he is gone on the weekends and holidays. She also added that this was during the time that she would be off from work.

I asked the lady if he was making his contribution to the household. She said, "Yeah, but that is not the point. He brings home good money when he works, but it is so god damn dangerous out there, especially with high unemployment and Reagan's cutbacks." I asked the lady if her man was happy being a cabbie. "He likes the freedom of the job," she replied. I told the lady that I understood! I also told her that my girlfriend rides my back continuously about getting out and I always tell her that is my ultimate goal. I told the lady that this type of work gets in your blood and it becomes hard to shake.

It is a big difference having ready cash in your pocket at the conclusion of your shift, rather than waiting weekly or bi-weekly for a cut up check! I told the lady that I don't know about her man but I'm definitely going to walk away and hopefully never have to look back! At the woman's destination, she said that she was going into this bar, have a couple of drinks in order to relieve her tension. While closing the door, she told me that she wants him out of this line of work immediately!

Most cab drivers are plain people who will let you know where they stand. The reasons they wind up in this profession are as diverse as the number of people who drive cabs. Many will say they cannot work for others. Many were laid off or fired from their jobs. Others will simply say that being a cabbie is a means to an end. They have other goals in life. The drivers make their own decisions. Cabbies love the freedom of going where they want to, picking up who they want to, or making their own hours. Whatever the reason, they are basically equal, and their primary objective is to make that **"BUCK."**

Most cabbies have the same objectives; some however, as in any walk of life, are better achievers than others. This stems from sensible hustling, salesmanship, diplomacy, showmanship, wit, financial pressures, perseverance, family responsibility, and goal setting.

It was about 11 p.m. on a rainy evening, at the intersection of Payson and Baltimore Streets, when this black lady got into the cab and requested to be transported somewhere down Ritchie Highway into the county. While driving, the lady stated that once she got home, she would have to go in the house concerning my money. She asked, "Is that okay?" I replied, "What am I to say if you don't have my money on you?"

At the lady's house, she left the cab and said she would be right back. About five minutes later, the lady came to the screen door and requested me to come into the house. Once inside, she stated that she had left a $20.00 bill on the kitchen table and that her daughter must have taken it. She then showed me this American Express check along with her driver's license and asked could I cash it. I said, "Lady, I am a cab driver. I don't cash or accept checks."

Then I advised the lady that I would take her up on Ritchie Highway with the check. We went to about five different places and they were either closed or they wouldn't cash it. At this point, the bill was over eight dollars. I said, "Miss, do you think that you could borrow the money from some neighbors?" She told me, "No, borrowing from neighbors is a bad practice."

Her remarks angered me. I said, "Lady, this is a jailable offense. I have been patient with you up to this point, but I want my money." She replied, "Then I guess that you'll have to put me in jail. I'm not borrowing money from any neighbors." She revealed that she was a home owner with her name on the mailbox and that she definitely wasn't going anywhere for eight dollars and some change.

After returning to the lady's house and checking out the mailbox, I gave the lady my calling card and told her that I expected my money to be mailed to me by Friday. I also copied her name and address from her driver's license and asked her for the phone number.

It took me thirty days and threatening phone calls to get my money from this lady. At one point, I threatened to go down there and break out eight dollars worth of windows if I didn't receive my money by a certain date.

Finally, I talked to her husband. He stated that she was a card gambler and that he would pay me whenever I was in the vicinity. One evening my lady friend and I were returning from Annapolis and I decided to stop pass and get my money. The husband was in and he gave me a $10.00 bill. For all the trouble that I had to go through, he should have given me $50.00. You may not know it, but cab drivers are a special breed and have to put up with a helluva lot of bullshit from people!

* * *

I picked this lady and her three children up at Park Circle. As she entered the cab, I could see that something *was under her coat. I felt secure due to the fact that the lady was with her children. I asked her what she had under her coat and she showed me a butcher's knife that was about twelve inches long. I asked, "What are you doing with that knife, Miss?" She stated that she was going to kill the children's father and that bitch that he is laying with. Then she stated that she wanted his children to witness the incident. I said, "Miss I know that you aren't serious." The woman didn't reply. I drove in the vicinity of Mondawmin Shopping Center. The lady didn't see what she was looking for, so we returned to Park Circle. After the lady paid the fare and while exiting, I told her that I hope that she wouldn't do anything that she would later regret.*

* * *

Bidded on a call in the vicinity of Baltimore and Fulton. I was dispatched to the unit block of North Fulton Avenue. Two young hillbillies entered the cab and instructed me to take them to the 5500 block of Old York Road. En route they told me that they were going to pick up their oldest brother who was handicapped. When we arrived at the location, they went inside and returned with all of these smelly clothes and requested that I open the trunk. After opening the trunk, they kept coming out of the house with all kinds of shit. I said, "Hey! What do you think this is a moving van or something?"

One of the brothers stated, "What difference does it make as long as you get your money?" I told him that this cab is my business and it makes a lot of difference to me. I stated that if you want this to be a moving van, then it will cost you $20.00, now! They talked it over, then one of the brothers went into his pocket and gave me the $20.00. Man, you would actually have had to have been there to witness how much shit was placed into the trunk and backseat of the cab! Then to top it off, this Sherlock Holmes character with a pipe in his mouth entered the cab and talked illogical shit all the way to his destination.

At the intersection of North and Fulton Avenue, a black man flagged me down. He requested that I wait at the intersection for a minute. He went into the bar and a moment later a white man about 25 years old came out of the bar and entered the backseat of the taxi. He told me to take him to the Hilton Hotel in downtown Baltimore. I could detect that this man was from New York or somewhere north. I wondered how he wound up in a black bar on North and Fulton Avenues.

He got to talking and commented on that being a rough neighborhood. My reply was that it's okay. He told me that he was from out-of-town and asked where he could find a decent place for him and his lady to eat at this time of evening. He also inquired about the ship that was docked in the harbor that was a restaurant. I advised him that the ship had been moved somewhere for repairs. I informed him that Harbor Place had some nice places to eat, and I thought they served until midnight. I told him that if he enjoyed seafood, Phillip's was supposed to be the best place down there.

When we arrived at the Hilton Hotel, the meter fare read $2.70. The man gave me a $20.00 dollar bill and requested me to wait for him. He told me not to take off and there was more where that came from. About 15 minutes later, he returned to the taxi with his lady. He told me to take him to this Phillip's place. When I approached Harbor Place, he told me that the $20.00 was mine and requested me to wait until he returned. I instructed him that I would be parked in the service drive in front of the Pratt Street Pavilion. I had been driving for a total of ten and a half hours so the thought of waiting would certainly give me a break.

While I waited, I decided to call my lady friend and we talked for quite a while. I waited for this guy and his lady for approximately 1 hour and 15 minutes. Then I said to myself, "Fuck it" and left. My reasons were that I got $20.00 out of this man and that I had a tiring day. I had already made a considerable sum for that day and was satisfied. As long as I get some of the action, I'm happy!

Hey Cabbie

Picked this black woman up in front of Trailways Bus Station. She stated that she wanted to go somewhere in the Edmondson Village area. At the intersection of Fayette and Howard Streets, I observed this lady in need of a cab. I turned and asked my fare was it okay, her reply was, "Sure if she is going in the same direction." The lady stated that she was going in the vicinity of Baltimore and Franklintown Road. The night was extremely slow and I was frustrated over something, but I still wanted to go home with something.

At the destination of the closest fare, I must have been really preoccupied with something heavy on my mind because the lady was going to pay me when the other fare said give it to her and that she would pay the total amount at her destination. These were supposed to be different fares. However, my mind wasn't on cabbing and I didn't say anything. But the other lady was definitely playing a game on me! When the lady got to her destination, she gave me the $2.50 that the other passenger had given her and told me to take the remainder from the two bucks that she pulled from her pocketbook. I said, "Miss you must be kidding, I know that you know that it costs more than $1.50 from downtown to the village." I said, "I hope that you don't expect any change" and refused to give it to her. She opened the door and said to me in a sarcastic manner to have a good evening. I felt like saying, "Yea bitch," but I left it at, "Have a good evening."

* * *

It was late and I had a taste for a slice of pizza from the pizza joint across from the Greyhound Bus Terminal. While entering the pizza shop, this old man with a gray beard appeared from the vestibule of the next building and called to me. I thought he was a wine-o and went into my change bag to give him a quarter. Instead he said, "Mister I'm a sick man, have no money, and will you please take me to the hospital?" I thought of my father who had recently died and took pity on the man. I agreed to take him after getting my pizza because the thought crossed my mind that this could have been my father begging for help. When I returned to the cab, the man was waiting at the door. He took a seat and I transported him to Maryland General's Emergency Ward. I then said, "What's wrong with you man?" He said that he is a kidney patient and he had run out of medicine. At this point, the smell of shit overtook the cab. I just chucked my pizza out the window. At the hospital, the man stated, "May God Bless you." When the man was turning to get out the cab, I noticed that he had moved his bowels on himself.

* * *

I was en route to the garage on this particular evening, which was around 11 p.m. At the intersection of Chester and North Avenues, this black woman hollered to me from across the street. As the lady crossed the street, I could see that she was high off of something heavy. I started to pull off but hesitated to see where this lady wanted to go. She snatched the door open, took a seat and told me to take her to Grantley Street in Edmondson Village. The lady was definitely fucked up and I asked her if she had the fare. She replied that they would pay on the other end. My reply was, "Oh no they won't." I then asked the lady to get out of the cab. She stated that she wasn't going a "goddamn place." I said, "Look Miss, don't make it hard on yourself and get the hell out of here before I call the cops." She said, "Call the cops, you black motherfucker!" Then she said, "I got my rights and you got to take me where I want to go." I said, "Miss if you don't have any money. I ain't taking you anywhere." She said, "Oh yeah, we'll see when the rollers gets here." My reply once again, "Miss if you don't have my money ain't nobody gonna make me take you anyplace." I told her that the best that anybody could do is to report me to the Public Service Commission.
Moments later this little white female police officer approached the vehicle and asked, "What's wrong

cabbie?" My reply was, "This lady doesn't have money and I refuse to transport." The cop told the woman, "Get out of the cab for your own good before I have to lock you up."

She said, "Bitch lock me up, I don't give a fuck." After hearing what this woman said, the little policewoman got immediately on her radio and called for backups. When support arrived, she was once again asked to get out the cab on her own accord before they had to pull her out and place her under arrest. The chick said, **"Motherfucker, I got my rights and I ain't moving NOWHERES."** The woman was stubborn as a mule. The policewoman and policeman pulled her out. It was funny watching this shit. The policeman was doing most of the work and the policewoman was barely assisting. The woman was placed on the ground struggling. They handcuffed her and placed her under arrest. I felt sorry for her, but she made her own bed.

The female cop then asked for my name and address. I gave them the cab company's address. They said that they wanted my home address. I stated that I wasn't going to give them my home address and what they had was sufficient. The cop then told me that I had to be in court by 9 a.m. the next morning. I told the cop that this was my money-making season, Christmas week, and that he could forget that. I also advised that if they needed my testimony for a conviction, it was best for them to get a postponement. I then asked the cop was she finished with me, and I left. It felt kind of nice having the white man respond to do a black man's dirty work.

There are various methods that a cabbie uses in order to procure a "fare". He may cruise the main thoroughfares of the city while looking for the hand signal. He may listen for someone to scream, **"TAXI!"** or he may listen for a whistle, and there is just the plain old instinct in knowing when a person is in need of your services. Some other methods are the use of cab stands, regular work, and being radio dispatched.

The cabbie that hustles the streets has priorities and will screen individuals from the moment they flag up until the time they attempt to enter the cab. The basic concerns are if they are a threat to your life and are they able to pay the fare? To a degree, the decision can be made based upon the hour of the day, section of town, male(s) or female(s), dress, age, couples, and race.

After making a decision, some cabbies will take off before the fare places his hand on the door handle. Discrimination is a means of survival for a cabbie. If by chance someone you perceive to be an undesirable fare enters your cab, simply refuse to transport. The cabbie will hear complaints about reporting them to the Public Service Commission. My advice is to tell them to, "Be my guest." You are basically out there alone, and in this business "your survival is you". Other cabbies and cops will respond concerning a distress call from a cabbie, but in most instances it is too late!

I know that this is stereotyping people concerning race, sex, and destination, but what recourse do cabbies have regarding their safety? Experience is a good teacher so why give history a chance to repeat itself? Many of the older cabbies will only work the radio, thinking that the fares are longer and that if something happens it can be traced to its origin. When the sun goes down, most of the old-timers retire for the evening.

While driving a taxi, I basically look at everybody as the enemy. I always keep the rear left door locked, so that no one will enter on my blind side.

I picked up this black juvenile at the intersection of Park Heights and Woodland Avenues who wanted to go to Frankford and Moravia. When the juvenile entered it was dark and he took a seat in the back. I requested that he sit up front with me. He entered the front and placed something on the floor creating a clumping sound.

The ride across town took approximately twenty minutes. The juvenile was not saying anything for a while. He was eyeing me and I was eyeing him. Finally, he started commenting on the Christmas decorations on Moravia Road. The juvenile smelled like fish. I asked him if he had been around fish. He stated that he cooks at Laketrout, a fish restaurant in West Baltimore. He told me, "Niggers must eat a million pounds of fish a week."

After my suspicions were eased, I discovered that the bag on the floor contained shoes.

    To procure a fare some cab drivers will tease a prospective fare during inclement weather - rain, snow, hail, coldness - especially during the winter. While stopped in traffic, empty and observing freezing MTA patrons waiting for the bus, a cab looks mighty appealing to some patrons. Many citizens might opt to take a taxi. They observe the cabbie sitting in the hack looking comfortable with no jacket or sweater on. Many are indecisive, but after taking a last peek for the bus, they will make a decision before the traffic light changes. In the winter months, the streets are virtually empty after dark, and due to the city's crime problem, they want to get out of the cold and if possible, arrive home safely.

    Once a patron is seated, the ultimate goal is to get them to their destination safely, but while transporting them you try to help them relax and treat them with respect. Basically, people are very polite. Most will not smoke before requesting permission. On the other hand, smokers need that outlet while being transported between locations. Some will even ask if it is okay for them to take a taste. The reply is generally, "Sure as long as you are discrete about it."

Picked up a fare at Fulton and Reisterstown Road - a couple and two children. They requested to go to Two Guys on Belair Road. While I was driving, the children became really wild! They started fighting. Their mother had to sit between them. The mother was eating peanuts; I later found the evidence all over the back seat. The boy friend appeared to be an "intelligent drunk" by his conversation. Many people ask if it is okay to drink or smoke in the cab, but this was the first time after replying to the fare that it was all right that I actually witnessed someone pull out a fifth of Richard's and an eight ounce drinking glass from his overcoat pocket and pour himself a drink. His lady later drank some of the wine out of the bottle to wash the peanuts out of her mouth.

    During the nights, especially in the winter, ladies standing in lonely bus stops are overjoyed when an empty cab comes in view. Crime statistics show that people standing alone at bus stops are prime targets for mugging, robbery and purse snatching. Once they are seated safely in the cab, they talk of how scared they were standing on the lonely street corner. They talk of the sacrifices in hiring a cab, but they always say that they would rather scrape the money together than to be harmed. Some of these people actually carry weapons for their protection. When they have reached their destination, many like to have the cabbie wait until they are securely in their residence. This ounce of concern and security relieves the patron's anxieties.

You know that many people are actually petrified of the city's streets concerning crime. This social worker who was a passenger stated that when she goes in certain areas of the city, she either carries a knife or a pistol!

This lady got into the cab and she had an open knife in her hand. She was so nervous handling the weapon that she cut her finger closing it! She stated, "Mister, I'm sorry, but I am just scared standing on these corners by myself waiting for the bus." When the lady arrived at her destination and before exiting the cab, she once again opened the knife. She revealed that at times, undesirables would hang in and around her apartment building. She also stated that she feels like a helpless prisoner having to live in that place. "Mister," she stated, "these are hard times. I don't make much money. My hands are tied. I just can't afford to move anywheres else at this time." I waited until she safely entered the building.

If you are a good listener, you will never have to read the newspaper. Fares do not discuss, but **tell** you everything from local gossip or news, to sports, politics, national and international events. Many people are actually talking to themselves! The cabbie is in agreement and serves as a springboard for the patron's conversation. This type of conversational release is perhaps good therapy for the patron, and it makes the cabbie's day quick and interesting.

Being mannerly is of utmost importance. This is a biggie! Just saying "good afternoon," "good evening," "have a nice day," or referring to one as Mister, Miss, Mrs., Sir, Ma'am means so much to so many. They love it. Even if they get in with an attitude, this type of greeting soon relaxes them. It may sound like nonsense, but on a one to one basis it makes many people's day.

Positive reactions from the cabbie concerning his fares may make it appear that the cabbie is a "whore" for a buck. Positive reactions and politeness determines the size of the tip that the patron may leave. While driving, a cabbie should always anticipate jumps on the meter; this is additional money in his pocket. **Trips are never completed until the cab is dead stopped at the fare's final destination. The meter can always be positioning itself for that final jump! This is what the industry is all about "M-O-N-E¬Y."**

After being in the business, a cabbie is aware when a fare wants him to keep the change from a bill. Sometimes this back-fires and the patron will ask you for his dime or twenty cents. You feel like asking, "What are you going to do with a dime?" But it is their money and you learn to keep your mouth shut! Hustling nickels, dimes, quarters, and bucks add up fast to a cabbie, but who knows with the patron.

I was dispatched to this house in the 2900 block of Westwood Avenue. After waiting impatiently for ten minutes, this couple exited a particular house and entered the cab. The dude stated that he wanted to go to East Baltimore. En route, the dude requested that I make two stops, tying up my time even more. When we finally reached his destination, the meter fare was $4.95, including surcharge and charge for the call. The dude gave me a five dollar bill and told me, "Keep the change." I gave him the nickel back indignantly and suggested that he probably needed it more that I did. 'What are you," I asked, "the last of the big -time-spenders?"
*He said, "Solid." He put **his** nickel in his pocket and got out of the cab.*

* * *

I was hailed by this interracial couple at the intersection of North Avenue and Charles Street. They appeared to be of the lower socio-economic class. They told me to take them to the sub joint located at 33rd and Guilford Avenue. While en route, I really wasn't listening to their conversation. When we arrived at their destination, the black dude told the white chick, "Pay him." She let him get out of the cab before paying the fare. She said, "He gets mad when I tip people." She paid the fare, gave me a reasonable tip and said, "Goodnight."

Since I've been employed as a cabbie, the lady is absolutely right about some blacks and their tipping habits. Many of them, even if they have 'extra' money wouldn't give you a plugged-nickel for your services. I know that some reason for this is because most of these people are poor; however, at other times I believe that it is learned behavior.

In this business "time is money." Many people want to waste your time in talking about some superfluous gibberish after they have paid the fare. It is all right when the meter is running, but once the fare has been paid and you have received a tip, it is time to seek the next job. Time is definitely money.

A cabbie should be flexible concerning the fares of the poor, desperate, and the elderly. Many times the poor and elderly will say, "Take me as far as 'X' amount of dollars will go." Based upon the person's frankness and honesty, and the **gut feeling of the cabbie,** (providing that they have most of the fare) the cabbie should transport within a close proximity of their destination. It can always be made up on the next fare. Chances go around, and you may need a similar favor one day. The same applies to the desperate who may just be a little short of the exact meter fare.

Picked up this man in front of the downtown Hutzler's Department store. Before entering the cab, he asked, "how much will it cost to take me to Bethlehem Steel?"

"Which one?" I asked. "Sparrows Point yard." I replied, "About eight dollars." "I only got six-dollars. Could you please take me as far as the money will go," the man asked. He further stated, "I just got hired down the 'Point' three days ago. I had to borrow this money for lunch and transportation. I don't have any more, please Mister? Since I'm late my lunch is out anyway."

I asked, 'Why is that?" He replied, "I works fifty feet high on a structure over the water, and they will not let you off until your shift is over." I told him that was heavy. He said, "What am I gonna do. I gots to work somewhere." I sensed from talking to this guy that he was desperate and wanted to keep his job, so I decided to take him to work for whatever he had. After revealing my intentions, he stated that he may be able to get some money out of his foreman. He then stated that if he did not get the money, for me to come to some project for the balance. I gave him my name and the address of the cab company and told him to mail my money there.

Once we were on the grounds of the "Point" the man did not know where his clock house was located. When we found it, his fare was ten dollars and forty cents. Sparrows Point police would not allow me to drive the cab down to the work site. A policeman called down to the work site and they sent someone up for the man. The foreman also sent three dollars. The guy was pleased and really thanked me for transporting him all the way to work. I looked at it this way, the six plus three dollars is nine dollars more than what I had. Then again, the day was extremely slow.

* * *

Bidded on the call in the 2400 block of Lauretta Avenue. At that location, a black man about thirty years old entered the taxi. He had been drinking, but appeared to be in a good mood. He wanted to go to Cedonia. He got to talking about his $25,000 a year job at Bethlehem Steel and how he was embarrassed to be riding in a cab. He went on to state that he was helping someone who was having car trouble in West Baltimore, revealing that he and the person that he was helping became involved in an argument. He went on to state that he wasn't an arguing person so he just got his hat and left. He continued to state that he knew a lady on Lauretta Avenue, so he stopped past her place to use the phone. While driving to Cedonia the guy asked me to stop at the bar located at North and Fulton Avenues so that he could buy a bottle. He also asked me if I wanted something and I told him to get me a can of beer. At the location, the taxi fare read $3.50. When he returned to the cab, he asked me if I would turn the meter off and he gave me $6.50. My reply was, "Okay." After riding for awhile, I stated to the guy, "Don't you think you are getting over on me." I said, "Just for a record I'll turn the meter on at North and Charles and see what the fare comes to by the time we get to your destination."

He once again talked about some shit like how embarrassed he was riding a taxi home. I asked him, "What are you talking about? The best of people ride taxies."

At the intersection of Sinclair Lane and Edison Highway, I added the two fares and they exceeded the $6.50 given to me. At the location, the fare was $7.00. He then added the can of beer, which cost about 75 cents and stated that should cover the total cost of the trip. I said, "Hey man. I didn't ask you to buy me that beer." He really made a big deal of the beer that he had purchased for me. I didn't like this guy's attitude enough to be doing him a favor.

He told me that he had $5.00 and that he wasn't going to give that to anyone and that the $5.00 was going into his gas tank. He said, doubtingly, to put him out when I thought he had ridden $6.50 worth. I told him that he was past his limit. The man thought that he was calling my bluff. In front of K-Mart on Sinclair Lane, I abruptly made a "U" turn and told him, "This is it man!" I conveyed to him that he wouldn't have to worry about being embarrassed by arriving home in a taxi. His reply was that he had another 12 blocks to go and I revealed that it cost money to operate this vehicle.

Really, I do a lot of favors for people who don't have enough cash, but I just didn't like this guy's attitude or his approach.

At the intersection of North and Druid Hill Avenues I was hailed by this young lady carrying a baby. She entered the taxi and requested to be transported to Maryland General Hospital. Once the meter was turned on she asked me to drive her to the employee's entrance on the

Hey Cabbie

Howard Street side of the hospital. She further revealed that she would have to go into the hospital and get the money from her husband. After telling me this, she asked if it would be okay with me. My reply was that I guess that it would have to be okay if she didn't have any money. On Howard Street, I pulled over to the employee entrance. The lady and the baby departed and to this date, I've never seen the bitch. I kinda trusted her because she sounded so sincere and she was carrying a baby. I should have told the lady to leave her baby in the cab until she returned with my money. Depending on the circumstances, I probably will do that in the future.

Racing to get in front of other empty cabs regarding a cab procession along a busy thoroughfare is not always profitable. It is true that everyone is strictly in this business for himself but some cabbies have no tact whatsoever. They will fly down busy commercial streets, jump in front of you at a red light to procure a fare. There is basically no formal training for cabbies in this city, and many would not know what common courtesy to others in the industry means. But being first in line does not always get it. What makes people decide to hire a cab is a "mystery." Empty cabs will be directly in front and/or behind you and a patron will select you. Why? No one really knows! Maybe they have a screening procedure for the cabbies, or their decision to hail a cab was a spur of the moment thing. Patrons also approach cabs for hire from all angles. At times, you are just at the right place and at the right time.

Many cabbies are notorious liars to their peers, especially when they start bragging about what they have made on an exceptionally slow day. If one works his shift and is a seasoned cabbie, he knows what is out there and what is not. Some days during the summer months, you are lucky to have the man's money, more or less a profit.

The primary question that over fifty percent of the people will ask is "Have you ever been robbed?" Most cabbies hate to hear this question. Being robbed, stabbed, or shot in this business is a real healthy fear. Most cabbies will play the question down, but in reality they do not want to hear it. Some may say **"fear nothing but fear itself."** Some cabbies are armed! As patrons exit from the cab, many will say "be careful," and my reply is ". . . to the best of my ability, thank you."

Picked this chick up at Fulton and Baker Streets. She was a pleasant lady but her conversation annoyed me. It just did not sit well. She stated that she vowed never to ride in a taxi again. I asked why? She stated that her stepfather was a driver for Diamond and that he was killed while working last year in the vicinity of Cold Spring Lane and Reisterstown Road. I told her that I remembered the incident and asked her was anyone ever arrested for the crime. She stated that one person was now in custody.

She stated that three dudes were in the cab when he was robbed and killed. She also revealed that her stepfather was a big dude, about 6' 5" and heavy. She went on to say that most people would think twice before messing with him. She revealed that he did beat one of them with a chain, I said, "I wish that he had killed the bastards." She stated that the whole incident was a big mess. She revealed that after he was shot, the police responded to the house and told her mother that her husband was in an accident. They requested that she come to the hospital with them. The whole family went to the hospital with the mother. After the wife had found that her husband was dead, the children wanted to see him. She stated that her mother was a nurse and could take the condition of the body, but she did not want the children to see their father with blood all over his body and bullet holes in him. She kept saying that it was a big mess, and she was glad when the funeral was over. She revealed that there must have been a "million" cabs in the funeral procession, stating that taxi representation was from every county in the state. It was sad hearing what this lady revealed about her stepfather, especially since I am a cabbie.

To the best of my knowledge, cab associations or companies operate on the owner/operator or lease/operator system in Baltimore City. They do not operate on a commission basis. Both systems have their advantages. The commission system consists of a 40-60% split, forty percent to the driver and sixty percent to the MAN. On a slow day, the operator always goes home with something, and on a good day, he will steal before giving it all to the MAN. The process of stealing is not turning the meter on. This is also called high-flagging.

The lease system, otherwise known as the "nut," prevents stealing from the man. The owner establishes a set price per shift and gets his money no matter what the business is bearing. Regarding the "nut," when the business is out there, you make money. Some days it is not worth the operator's while to work, and if you do not pay for a given shift within a prescribed period, you may find yourself without a job.

Only the strong survive in this industry. This is a dog-eat-dog job, profession, trade, or whatever you want to call it. In order for a cabbie to make it, he must be a damn good salesman. At times, ego-tripping, the product that he is selling is himself and the efficiency of his cab. Sometimes that can be quite heavy dealing with the public.

> *I was cruising in the Highlandtown section and was hailed by two dirty white juveniles at the intersection of Patterson Park and Eastern Avenue. They instructed me to take them to Madison Avenue in the vicinity of the Greyhound Bus Station. I advised them that Madison Street was located around the bus station. They asked would that be about the 300 block. My reply was yes. One of the youths then asked, "Hey pal, do you know anything about that juvenile home on Madison Street?"*
> *I said, "No."*
> *En route to their destination, I could sense from their conversation that they hardly ever left Highlandtown. From observing these juveniles in the rearview mirror, they kept eyeing me, and I knew that they were scheming up something. They just kept whispering.*
> *When we got to the downtown area, they instructed me to drive north on Howard Street and to stop at the northeast corner of Madison and Howard Streets. After they exited the cab, I observed them going to this house where these winos were gathered. The guys called for this girl, who later stuck her head out of a second floor window. The girl threw her shoes out of the window, climbed out, and*

she was hanging upside down by one hand and a foot, dangling in the air like a dirty piece of linen. The two youngsters on the ground attempted to grab one of her limbs, but they could not reach her. They asked one of the winos to assist them.
The unsteadiest of this motley crew volunteered his assistance. He was so drunk that he could hardly stand up. He climbed to the top step of the dwelling, reached out and grabbed the young girl by her feet. She was now dangling precariously from the ledge of the second floor by one hand, a wino clinging to her feet. They commenced to sway back and forth, the drunk on the verge of losing his balance, the girl about to lose her grip. It was like being at the circus, but it was hardly amusing. In a way it was humorous, I wanted to laugh, but I couldn't. I was afraid that the girl was going to fall backwards and 'bust' her head open. She managed to maneuver her body up against the building, how I don't know, but she resembled a huge fly crawling up the wall attempting to free itself from the grasp of a spider. From this position she was then able to jump down to the top step where the committee of winos and delinquents were stationed to break her fall. Once she was on the ground, all three ran towards the taxi. I said, "What do you think this is, a get-away-car? Don't you know that this makes me an accessory to a crime?"
"Don't worry pal," one of the juveniles stated, "we'll make it worth your while."
"Well, my while is twenty-five bucks."
"OK, pal, just take us around the corner." I transported them to Cathedral and Read Streets as fast as it was possible. I got my twenty-five bucks and got the hell out of the area.

* * *

It was about six p.m. one weekday, when this woman and her children flagged me at the intersection of Goodnow and Sinclair Lane. She said, "I know that this is going to sound ridiculous, but I only want you to drive me a half block to the bank and get in the drive-in line."

I said, "Miss, I've been doing this type of work long enough for nothing to sound ridiculous. Why can't you just walk up to the window?"

"These are the bank rules after the front door's been closed for over-the counter transactions." After the woman had transacted her business, she requested that I take her to the #44 bus stop on Frankford Avenue and Sinclair Lane.

"Where are you going Ma'am?" I asked.

"Reisterstown Plaza," she replied.

"Well," I said, "you can wait for the #44 if you want to, but you know how slow it is. I'll tell you what," I continued. "I'll take you to the Plaza for ten bucks."

She said, "I'll tell you what, you'd better take these three bucks for that four-block trip and be satisfied." I guess she told me!

* * *

This black guy who had a good "load on" flagged me at Milton Avenue and Federal Street. He wanted to go somewhere in the Forest Park section of the city. Before moving or turning the taxi meter on, I asked, "Do you have any money?" He replied, "I got in the cab didn't I."

"What does that mean," I asked. "Plenty of people get in here with no money. If they are sober and cry a good enough story, I will transport them. Now back to you, you are drunk or have been drinking, and if you don't have the money, I'm sorry but you will have to find other means."

At this time the man showed me some money. "Do you tell this to all of your customers?" He asked drunkenly.

"No, only to those who had been drinking and appear to be the least bit full of shit. I don't care to have them waste my time, gas, and enjoy my air conditioning due to their condition, if I can't see the money." I quickly added that this reaction comes from experience, "It is almost worthless to call the police for taxi fare problems. In the

past, I have had people locked up, gone to court, and still did not get my money."
He then said, "You'll never make any money that way."
My reply was, "Oh! I do all right!"

Today the inner city or poorer people comprise a major portion of the business for the cab industry. Yet, how does the industry deal with this group? The first day or first working day of every month is known as ***Mother's Day.*** This is when those in need receive welfare relief checks.

Baltimore has a lot of people in need! The checks are distributed through the mail. These assistance checks put a lot of money into the system. They contribute to a heavy influx in most inner-city businesses. The establishments that flourish during this time of the month are food markets, banks, cabs, check cashing places and apparel stores.

A negative side effect of this influx of money is that the crime rate increases, and illicit drugs are readily available. There is more money in the system during the first week of the month than any other time.

The taxi services are very busy! Many people spend their money as fast as they get it. Most relief people believe in living extremely well until the money is gone. Many businesses survive off the first of the month's action. Most cab operators will concentrate their work schedule on the beginning of a month. If you go to any cab garage during the beginning of the month, one will notice that the majority of the fleet is on the street.

Supplementary Social Insurance checks (SSI) come out on the third or third work.ing day of the month. These checks are issued to the elderly and those with physical and/or mental handicaps. Checks for foster care parents come out on the eleventh of the month.

Many welfare recipients want to do ridiculous things when they hire your services. A biggie would be waiting for them while they go into a rip-off place or bank to cash their checks. They want to tie up your time and reward you with nothing extra! Everybody is aware of check day in the ghetto.

Picked up this fare at Park Heights and Belvedere. He told me that he had three stops to make. First he wanted to go somewhere on Cold Spring Lane, so that he could get his check. Next he wanted to go to the Seton Apartments to pick up a friend. Then he told me to take him downtown to a bank on Saratoga and Howard Streets. At the bank, I was requested to wait until he cashed his check. I asked, "Do you have my fare?"

"I'll have it when I cash my check," he stated. The man's friend stayed in the cab. The first of the month is a money making week, and it is not to my advantage to wait. In this business, you make your money with wheels rolling and the flag down! The man took an extremely long time. When he returned, the fare read fourteen dollars and some change. The man gave me exactly what was on the meter. I told him, "You have one helluva nerve, tying up my time waiting for you." Also, "Where is my tip?"

"I'm sorry buddy," the fare said, giving me five bucks. This type of behavior is typical of welfare recipients; most of them always want a lot of service for nothing!

The Public Service Commission of Maryland has allowed Baltimore City 1035 taxi permits. Out of those 1035 permits, approximately 935 actually operate on the streets daily. Regarding the 935 vehicles, almost fifty percent can be classified as unfit and unsafe for public transportation. The life of a vehicle as a taxi is five years. This life span can be shortened by a serious accident.

The Public Service Commission holds permits for about 3000 licensed hack operators. The majority are part-timers contributing to about 600 full time employees with seven cab companies. Out of the seven companies, six of them are associations, meaning individual owners using the same benefits under one established name. The other company is independently owned.

A cab company's reputation is known by its professionalism, vehicle cleanliness, and prompt service regarding telephone work. When a company becomes branded as not dependable, people stop calling them for service. This contributes to their negative reputation and a cut in somebody's revenue. A cab company's nobility is known by its response to telephone service and politeness.

Bidded on a call in the vicinity of Eutaw Place and Dolphin Street. I was dispatched to 1499 Eutaw Place.

While blowing the horn, a couple approached the taxi and I asked were they from 1499 Eutaw Place and they replied, "Yes." I then asked were their names Evans. They said, "That's right." They directed me to drive them to the 400 block of North Eutaw Street. At their destination, they were charged the meter fare plus twenty-five cents for the call. After they alighted, the dispatcher called me and asked what happened to 1499 Eutaw Place. I advised him that I had just let them out in the 400 block Eutaw Place. The dispatcher figured that they were still in the cab and asked me to ask them their names. I once again advised him that they had departed. I advised the dispatcher that I would respond back to 1499 Eutaw Place. What really happened is that the bastards lied and stole the taxi. This happens quite often.

The elderly depend upon the cab system. Many do not drive and depend on cabs to take them to hospitals, churches, doctor's offices, food markets, and banks. This segment of the city's population also contributes to a lot of revenue to the industry. Some cab companies have government contracts to transport the indigent, disabled, and elderly primarily to and from hospitals.

Bidded on a call in the 2300 block of North Calvert Street. At that location, this elderly lady about 70 years old entered the taxi. She was black and had a couple of teeth in her mouth, a shopping bag on her arm, and she used a cane. She wanted to be transported to a beauty parlor in the 1800 block of West North Avenue. At the intersection of North and Charles Street, I was hailed by a black male about 45 years old. I inquired if he was going west and he stated that he wanted to go somewhere in the Pimlico area. Once this guy was seated in the taxi, his conversation revealed that he was one of those "Jesus freaks", plus he was intoxicated. He started annoying the elderly lady by calling her sweetheart and doll-baby. He also told her that she didn't have to worry about the fare, that he would take care of it. I intervened by saying that I didn't know him and to let the lady pay her own way. The lady insisted that she pay her fare and for the drunk to leave her alone. At the lady's destination, I apologized for picking up the other fare and helped the lady out the cab and onto the curb.

When I returned to the cab, the drunk stated that he wanted to go to the 4200 block of Park Heights Avenue. He then said once he got there, he was going to kick his daughter's ass for stealing his money. He then requested that I stop at the liquor store at Reisterstown Road and Gwynn Falls Parkway so that he could purchase a bottle. I parked at the bus stop. He exited the vehicle and started toward the entrance of the liquor store. Instead of going into the place, he went about two yards to the left of the entrance, pulled out his stuff in broad daylight and peed up against a telephone booth. He then entered the liquor store, returned to the taxi with his bottle, and gave me a $5.00 bill for the trip. As I continued on to his destination, his conversation was solely about the Lord and his children. The $5.00 that the drunk had given me at the liquor store was more than enough for the trip.

* * *

Bidded on a call in the vicinity of Hopkins Hospital and was dispatched to the main entrance. When I arrived at the Wolfe Street entrance, a lady with a child about 11 years old approached the taxi with the child in a wheelchair. She asked if I was there for her. My reply was yes. I had to exit the taxi, to physically lift the child out of the chair and place her in the taxi. The lady stated that she wanted to be transported to the 500 block of University Parkway. En route to the passenger's destination, I started to observe the child, noticing that she was motionless and that she just existed as a living being in this world. The mother and I became involved in a conversation and she stated that her child had cerebral palsy. She told me that they were from Sweden and had come to Johns Hopkins Hospital in America because of its reputation in the field of medicine around the world. Looking at the child in the backseat, she looked so sweet, precious, and innocent. At that precise moment, I started thinking of my daughter who had been diagnosed as having traces of cerebral palsy in her system. To date, this basically affects her speech only. Her mother and I are still in search for the proper techniques in teaching our child to overcome her speech problem. After observing this child in my taxi, who also had cerebral palsy, I am really thankful that my child's problem is of a milder nature. My child does have problems with her peers in today's cruel world because of her speech, but believe me, I've observed living evidence that her condition could be so much more severe. I am thankful that her problem is mild and that she is functional in life. As a parent, I know how this lady feels. I know that she is thankful that she has a child, but in a reality I know that she wants to see signs of improvement. The child could not maneuver her main body functions, yet it was rather evident that her mother loved her dearly!

Driving a cab makes one aware of how important it is to be in good health. It is worth more than all the money in the world! You cannot buy a leg, arm, eye, hand, or other part. These and other parts of the anatomy are priceless! Many times I transport the terminally ill or incapacitated people to and from the hospitals. Believe me, at times it is rough listening to some of these people's stories.

I bidded on a call in the vicinity of Hopkins Hospital. The dispatcher asked if I could handle a wheelchair. My reply was yes. He instructed me to go to Wolfe Street side of the hospital and meet a man in a wheelchair. At the entrance, I met this man in a chair who had no legs. I exited the cab and rolled his chair to the right front door of the taxi, getting in as close as possible. The man was very independent, lifting his legless body into the cab. After placing the chair in the trunk, he instructed me to take him someplace on Federal Street. It appeared peculiar not to have to ask this man to move his legs while turning the taxi meter flag. I asked what had happened to his legs. He stated that he was a diabetic, and they had to keep cutting his legs a little higher. The man stated that he practically lives in hospitals. Although this man was handicapped, his spirits and humor were excellent. When I arrived at this man's destination, he told me that he was happy to be alive. This got me to thinking that at times life can really be rough but it's the only thing you've got.

* * *

This white distinguished looking gentleman about 55 years old entered the cab in front of the Wolfe Street entrance of Johns Hopkins Hospital. After the man was seated in the taxi, he stated that he had just had a "new lens" installed in his right eye from the Wilmer Institute of the hospital. He said that he felt like a new man! He appeared in high spirits and his personality was super. He stated later that he had had cataracts removed from both eyes last year.

We talked about the cold weather and he stated that he rather liked the coldness. He told me that it gets much colder in Pennsylvania and Michigan where he used to live. Once we arrived at his destination, the gentleman paid his fare and told me to give him a minute to get out the taxi because his right leg was artificial. I thought to myself, if one would have looked at this man, they would have never known that anything physically was wrong with him. The man was really **the bionic man.**

I had just left the cab garage, in search or my first fare and was approaching 25th Street and Greenmount Avenue. At that location this black lady called "Taxi," faintly from across the street. I noticed that she was walking with the assistance of a cutoff broom handle and had a sheer yellow plastic shopping bag on her arm as she approached the cab. Once she entered, the lady said that she wasn't old, but lately she had been through some hard times. I guess the lady was about twenty-five years old but from her appearance and the look in her eyes she looked to be about fifty. The lady had this sincere look in her eyes and said, "Mister I don't have any money, will you take me to the 1000 block of East 20th Street. The lady then pulled her skirt about six inches up her left leg *and showed me this nasty looking grease burn about two inches square. It was the worst thing that I had ever seen on a human being. It was oozing, scabby, and diseased looking.*

After seeing that mess on the lady's leg, I told her, "Sure, I'll give you a lift." I asked the lady what had happened to her leg. She stated that she was cooking some spare ribs and the hot grease splashed on her leg as she was taking the pan from the oven. I asked why she didn't go to the hospital. She said that she was once burned in a fire and that she was never going through pain like that again. My reply was, "Miss, if you don't take care of that leg immediately, either you are going to lose the leg or die from infection."

She said that she would rather die than go through that pain. At her destination, she wanted to thank me with a hand shake. I told her that a verbal reply was sufficient. I then said that I would take her to a hospital if she liked. She said, "Thanks," but she was afraid and wanted her sister to go with her.

If one would ask a middle class cab rider why he spends "X" amount of dollars weekly in cab fares, he would tell you to compare the expenses of owning a vehicle (car payments, gas, insurance, maintenance, and traffic tickets) to riding a cab, who would come out cheaper? Some people say that their nerves cannot stand what a driver has to put up with. If you would ask them what about the convenience of being able to move when you are ready, they would respond by saying, once you get a reputation with a company as a regular rider, it is no problem. They would conclude by saying that it has its advantages and disadvantages.

Strippers, fags, and prostitutes travel by cabs and are fairly good tippers. The strippers on the "Block" are taxied to and from work daily. They say that they make good money and have no need for a car. This city has a heavy fag population and a lot of them live around the central section of the city and use taxi services continuously. Driving is probably too masculine for them. Prostitutes take their tricks to rooms or hotels once they have scored. These people are a big market for the business.

Picked up this 30 year old white man at North Avenue and Charles Street. I was stopped in traffic, in the center lane, which forced the man to run out to the taxi. He requested to be transported to the big numbers on Belair Road.

When the man entered the taxi, I observed that he was not all man! He carried himself as one, but one could see that he possessed feminine tendencies. He started asking about my day and if I was heavy into sports. He then commented on my slender body. The guy or gay was riding up front and at this point threw his left arm over the seat. I just said to myself, "What is next?"

He observed my advertising directory and asked, "Is this you?" I replied, "Yes." He told me that he had been employed by IBF for the past fifteen years. After looking at him, I told him that he could not be any older than thirty. He told me that he started working for IBF when he was fifteen and attended college at night. From talking to this guy, one could see that he was extremely intelligent. From the start, this guy had been trying to hit on me. At his destination on Belair Road, he requested that I wait for him. When he returned, he asked me if I wanted to stop off and have a beer. My reply was that I had just started driving and that I never stop until I had at least made the man's money. He then requested me to drive him to the 1800 block of Calvert Street. En route we passed Greenmount Avenue Cemetery and I started talking out loud. I was saying that one day I really would like to go up in that place to observe and read the tombstones. He responded by saying that he would go into the cemetery with me. My answer was, "Naw man, I do not want to go up into any cemetery with you," and I started laughing. At the Calvert Street address, I was once again requested to wait. He returned with a jacket and stated that since I did not want a beer with him, to take him downtown. While heading downtown, he asked, "Do you fuck around?"

I asked him what he meant, laughing to myself. He stated that he was bi, and that he wanted to get into something.
I replied, "Hey man, I am sorry but I just cannot help you." Downtown his final fare was $11.00. He gave me $15.00 and left from the cab sadly. I thought to myself, maybe the poor guy will find a trick downtown.

People who are sneaking out on their spouses will use the taxi services to transport them to cheap motels. They either go out on Washington Boulevard or Pulaski Highway looking for accommodations. If they have vehicles, they probably do not want to be identified by them.

I bidded on this call in the 1800 block of East 30th Street. This chick entered the taxi dressed in a very revealing top and a pair of shorts. She told me that she wanted to go to the Holiday Inn downtown.

En route to the Holiday Inn, I was observing her in my rear view mirror putting on her make-up mud, fixing her nails, and getting herself in order for the trick that she was meeting. I've been a taxi driver long enough to know ladies for hire! Once we arrived at the Holiday Inn, she requested that I wait while she went inside to get my money. I requested that she leave her pocketbook in the taxi until she returned. She so complied. She returned to the taxi stating that he wasn't there and asked if I wouldn't mind waiting until his arrival. I then asked if I had any alternative, her reply was that she did not have any money. I then stated that I guess I would have to wait. She told me that the trick had big paper and that I would be treated well! I asked could she get $20.00 for my time. She stated, "No problem."

About twenty minutes had elapsed, and I then asked her where was this guy. Revealing to her that it was WELFARE WEEK and that there was plenty money on the streets. I could see that she was getting nervous by the minute and she asked me to "be cool."

The lady observed her trick pulling into the parking lot seconds later. This Italian guy walked around to the taxi, *said something to the lady, and asked me how much was the fare. I revealed the meter read $8.00 plus waiting time. The bastard gave me a ten spot and told me to keep the change. The chick got out of the taxi, said something to the dude, but he never came across with any additional cake. I was pissed but what recourse did I have? I started the taxi and wandered on in search of the next fare.*

* * *

Bidded on this call in the 2500 block of Eutaw Place. This black chick about 23 years old entered the taxi with a suitcase and about three bundles of clothes. She started cursing, stating that, "I am tired of that motherfucker accusing me of giving my pussy away." She said, "Just for spite, I am going to give somebody my pussy tonight." I informed her that she did not have to look any further for a participant. She told me to take her out to Druid Hill Park. I informed her that we didn't have to go to the park; that I had an apartment on the Drive. She said, "Let's get a quart of beer and go to your place." I purchased the quart of beer and later parked the taxi in the rear of my apartment building.
Before she exited the cab, she asked if I was still going to charge her the meter fare. I said, "Of course not!" Once inside we drank the beer, smoked a joint and got into bed. She stated that she would like to work me over and started licking, sucking, and kissing me all over my body. We did our number, she then put her clothes on and we left the apartment. I transported her somewhere on West Lafayette Avenue. We exchanged telephone numbers and thanked each other.

Cabbies have various strategies pertaining to driving patterns and how they procure their fares. Cab drivers work and operate individually, and it is impossible to say how smart they work! But the days of the week do have their uniqueness. Monday through Friday (during season) follows the same pattern. Cab season in Baltimore is basically from September to May. When it is hot, this is a tough business.

Good business is during the rush hour traffic 7:00-10:00 a.m. in the morning and 3:00-6:00 p.m. in the evening. Between 10:00 a.m. - 3:00 p.m. is hospitals, schools and senior citizens' work; 6:00-8:00 p.m. is relatively slow during the dinner hours; and 8:00-10:00 p.m. is slow but steady business. Telephone work is to the cabbie's advantage. After 10:00 p.m., people who have night jobs start going to work. Around 11:00 p.m. strange people and the night owls hit the streets. This is when you really start screening fares! At midnight the evening shift is going home. During season, Friday's business is good all night long - well up until after the bars are closed. Saturday is basically market day for many. The trips are short and concentration is around the core of the city. As the day progresses, people start hitting the streets. Saturday is the day that many shoppers contribute to good business in commercial shopping centers and districts. Then the evening shows a somewhat romantic flavor because we transport a lot of couples to places of entertainment.

Most cab drivers take-off on Sundays and this minimizes the number of cabs on the street. Up to about 2:00 p.m., your biggest market is churchgoers. This is a very relaxing day to work. It is a pleasure to drive, traffic is light. In the evenings, men are taking their ladies to movies or people are making social visits. Around 8:00 p.m., people who are visiting the town are transported to bus stations for their return trip home. Holidays follow the Sunday schedules. The day before a holiday is similar to Saturdays.

On a slow day, if you have noticed, cabbies will be sitting in their vehicles while parked on Howard Street downtown or around Lexington Market; their behavior is like vultures preying on a catch. Business is slow all over town and cabbies are looking for that "BUCK." On a slow day when a cabbie is riding empty, he projects a stone face looking from left to right in search of that fare! They also will bid on calls miles away and hope that they will not get scooped.

People complain about cabs not being in abundance around outlying areas of the city. A cabbie's money is made around the center city. For the most part, the only time he is around the boundary lines is when a fare takes him there. This is why city people who live around the line call for county cab service. A cabbie makes money by keeping the back seat occupied at all times and this is apt to be done in the center-city where conditions are crowded and people need transportation. Whereas transporting patrons to outlying areas, the cabbie has to deadhead back to the downtown section empty.

Picked this white man up at the intersection of Eastern Avenue and Broadway. He told me to take him to Kavanagh's Bar located in the 300 block of West Madison Street. It was evident that the man was drunk before he got into the cab. After he heard me talk, he asked me where did I teach and if I was doing this as a part-time job. I informed him that it is **"ROUGH"** *out here and that this was it! His reply was "Oh come on." I told him that I was qualified to do other things but presently was not able to find my type of work.*

At the bar, he paid his fare, gave me a dollar tip, and told me to return in about 45 minutes. He told me that he lived in Lutherville and that he was going to take a cab home. Most cab drivers would return for a fare from downtown to Lutherville, it's about a $10.00 job. I returned about an hour later. He came out, told me that he was talking to his grandchildren, and to give him a couple more minutes. I told him, okay but that I was going to come in and have a drink on him.

While in the bar, I met the bartender and his wife who was the waitress. They told me that they were really actors but this was their sideline until they could get into their profession. **The waitress stated that I should write a book about the characters that I encounter in my cab. I responded that I had the raw data but that I had never had the time to put it together. She replied "Yeah, I bet that you have some good stuff."**

With the help of the bartender, we finally got this patron out to the cab. He told me to take him to Fred's Bar located on York Road in the Govans section of the city. Once we were inside this white blue collar bar, this man introduced me (with my black face) to some of his old friends as his grandson. They just laughed but made no comments. He had two shots of whiskey and I had beer. He was so drunk that he wanted to kiss one of his friends whom he hadn't seen for years. The guy kind of pushed him away. The man was beginning to waste my time and I told him that I had to turn the cab in by 11:00 p.m. It took awhile but I finally got him out of the bar. He told me to stop him pass the Little Tavern in Towson so that he could purchase some hamburgers and coffee for us.

After we ate, I transported this intoxicated gentleman to this beautiful house in Lutherville, just north of the Beltway. From the bar to his house, I guess I got about $18.00 out of this man. Before leaving the cab, he gave me another $5.00. From his conversation, the man was intelligent and good people. The man was drunk but he really had a heart and compassion for others.

* * *

Picked up a white female juvenile on St. Mary Street who wanted to be transported to Randallstown. Once the girl was seated in the cab, I could sense that she was high. I inquired and she stated that she had just smoked an excellent roach. We got involved in a conversation about her family. She revealed that her mother put her out when she was 15. She went to live with her father for awhile but moved because he had no heat. I told her that was a problem! The juvenile told me that she was 16 and now living with a 27 year old man. She also revealed that she was going to sleep with a dude in Randallstown and try some of his drugs. After she paid her fare, she told me that she survives by hustling weed. I wished her luck with her future!

* * *

This black chick whom I later learned to be a lesbian whistled for me in the 500 block of South Broadway. She was coming from a show bar and requested to be taken to Brooklyn. I asked, "Brooklyn down off Patapsco Avenue?" And she stated, "Yes." That was a very peculiar request because you don't get very many blacks going to that section of town. En route we became involved in a heavy conversation concerning homosexuality. She dressed as a half stud and half woman, if you know what I mean. She stated that she had been this way as long as she could remember. She then revealed that she screws men but that it was rare and that there was nothing to it. This lesbian was doing most of the talking, asked me if I was married, how many children did I have and did I have a girlfriend.

After answering those questions, she revealed that she had fucked a few cab drivers. My ears perked up, I said, "Oh yeah!" I then asked her would she like to give me some! She said, "You're kinda cute, sure, if I don't have to pay the fare." I replied laughingly, "I am not going to fuck you and make you pay the fare too." Saying to myself, that it would be nice if I could get it!

At this point I was driving south on Hanover Street approaching the bridge in the industrial area known as Port Covington. Right before the bridge, I made a left turn and went back by the grain elevators. I selected some dark isolated area by the water and got in the back seat of the cab. The lesbian had her pants off, laying over the backseat with one leg bent up on the seat and other on the floor of the cab. I said, "Hey baby, I ain't quite ready; how about making me hard. This ain't the kind of fucking that I am used to and you don't turn me on just like that." Then the lesbian started yanking on my stuff. I said, "Even though you're a lesbian, you appear to be quite brutal." My stuff finally got hard, got on top of the chick and was getting ready to put it in when the smell of the chick's breath just turned me off! Immediately I came to my senses and started thinking how much of a dog that I was and stopped myself. She said, "What the fuck is wrong with you." I told her that she just didn't turn me on. I then started thinking about getting caught in this public taxicab with this lesbian and the repercussions that could follow. I guess the heavy alcohol smell on her breath contributed to my lust desires vanishing. I told the lesbian that she didn't have to worry about the fare.

As a cab driver, when leaving the garage, the main concern is being issued a functional piece of equipment with a good radio and a fairly accurate meter. These are the basic tools of the trade. A faulty vehicle, radio, or meter contributes to loss of time and money. A malfunctioning vehicle with stalling engine, bad brakes, or no lights endangers the safety of the cabbie and his fares. A decent radio contributes to a cabbie's profit and safety if something goes down. In this business, down time is money lost, or the absence thereof; and that is something that a cabbie does not have too much of to spare. The name of the game is to keep the wheels rolling, back seat occupied, and the flag down.

Once the cabbie has begun his shift, he is confronted with **FINDING THAT BUCK** and returning the equipment in the same condition that it left the garage. At times this can be difficult. This makes cabbing a lonely profession, and it contributes to the cabbie looking at everyone as the enemy. The administration of the cab industry is enemy number one. They always have the upper hand. If anything happens to the cab or if the rental money is short, the cabbie is "guilty as charged" until he proves himself innocent.

Some policemen will do a number on cabbies, knowing that they are out there hustling to make an honest living.

While driving south on Greenmount from North Avenue, I looked in my rear view mirror and noticed the flashing lights of a cop's car. The officer was motioning me to pull over to the right. **I pulled over, came to a halt and sat there wondering why this officer is fucking with me on such a busy day.** *He got out of his car and approached the cab on the driver's side. Before I could ask the officer why he was stopping me, he said, "I'm sick and tired of this goddamn shit from you ass-hole taxi drivers... stopping in the middle of the street picking up passengers."*

I wanted to ask **"Who me?"** *But this cop was red in the face, and I imagined that you probably could have fried an egg on his neck. From his approach one would think that the worst crime in the history of mankind had just been committed.*

"Give me your driver's license and registration," he demanded in a very nasty manner.

He took the license and registration and returned to his car. I looked in my rearview mirror and noticed that he was transmitting over his walkie-talkie. Moments later, he returned to the driver's side of the cab without a ticket book in his hand. He said, "Next time I'm going to give your fucking ass a goddamn ticket."

I thanked the cop for being lenient with me, but deep down inside I was revolted by his behavior. He showed no respect for me or for my passenger who was seated in the rear of the taxi. His approach from "jump" was totally wrong. He showed none of the professionalism as one of "Baltimore's Best." Some policemen are just nasty, and it is useless to attempt to reason with them.

Other cab drivers can also be your enemy. It makes no difference if they work for your company or not. Those that work for the same company will "scoop" you, which means that they will beat you to a fare that you bidded for over the radio. Others will pick up fares that were promised to you on the street. For instance, you are heading south when you are hailed by a fare on the north side of the street. You need to make a "U" turn in order to pick up the fare. While waiting for the traffic to clear so that you can make the turn safely, a fellow cab driver will hustle your fare before you can turn around in traffic. What can you do? You have been hustled!

Patrons are potentially your worst enemies. You have to use your mirrors, peripheral vision, wit, and conversation in an attempt to stay one step ahead concerning your safety or whatever.

The Public Service Commission is like a spy in disguise. They are supposed to enforce the taxi laws. Instead they follow cabs and hang around bus stations, trains and public toilets. Basically, they check, or they are supposed to check for taxi manifest violations. Everything on the manifest should coincide with the readings on the taxi meter. The cabbie has to be alert and prepared at all times with his defenses concerning the enemies. Anyone of these vehicles can contribute to loss of time and the privilege to hustle as a "cabbie." In this industry you learn to cover your ass quickly.

As a cabbie, you are confronted with and can expect just about anything from people after they tell you their stories and adventures about themselves. Some will attempt to exit the cab and substitute other tangibles for money. You may be offered marijuana, sex, food stamps, or stolen goods for the fare. Depending upon the value of what the fare has to exchange, sometimes with a slim possibility, it may be accepted. As a rule, however, a cabbie wants "money" and no substitutes. His employer will only accept United States currency to pay off his shift. The other tangibles will not pay the expenses.

> Picked up this black male on Route 40 West en route back to town. Once the man was seated in the taxi, I observed that he had a bag of meats. I figured he had probably stolen them. I asked whether or not he had caught a good supermarket sale or if he was in the meat business.
>
> "I am in the meat business," he replied. "I sell my merchandise for fifty percent less than the sticker prices."
>
> "Oh yeah!" What's the special today?" I asked. "Steaks and backfin crabmeat."
>
> When the guy got to his destination, his fare was three dollars and thirty cents. "I'll tell you what," I said. "Give me two steaks totaling about six dollars and sixty cents, less the fifty percent deduction instead of the fare."
>
> "You've got a deal brother," the man replied. The steaks paid for the fare. Later that evening, my lady and I had the steaks for dinner under candle light. They were delicious!

* * *

> Transported this lady somewhere in the Catonsville area. I had a taste for some ice cream, so I decided to stop at Baskin & Robbins located at Rolling Road and Route 40. While turning into the shopping center lot, I heard this dude holler but I didn't respond. While entering Baskins & Robbins, the dude ran up to me and asked would I take him over by Security Boulevard. My reply was, "Sure, after I get my ice cream."
>
> When I returned, he stated that he didn't have any money, but he did have three Maryland State Tic-Tac-Toe winners. I said, "Let me see them." They were "ligit," but

I told the man that I needed money and that this was an inconvenience. The dude stated that he had about $1.50 in silver. I told him that I would take the silver plus the lottery tickets. The fare ran about $4.00. The lottery tickets and money equaled about $7.50. People will give you just about anything for the fare.

* * *

While cruising in the 1800 block of West Lafayette Avenue, this lady flagged. She approached the taxi and asked would I transport her somewhere in the Forest Park section for food stamps. I asked, "How much in stamps?" And she stated, "Seven dollars worth."
I then asked, "Do you need identification for them to be honored." The lady asked, "Don't you know anybody who uses food stamps?" My reply was, "No." I said, "All right, I'll take you!" The fare was $2.50; the excess was a good tip.

* * *

I was stopped at the traffic light at Roland Avenue and 40th Street when this black dude ran over and said, "I am glad to see you." From the direction that he had approached, he must have been leaving the Rotunda Shopping Center. He told me to take him to North and Division Street. I made a right turn and drove south toward the Falls Road entrance to the interstate. The trust that these people have in cabbies is unbelievable. While driving, this guy stated that he had a good day and pulled out about fifteen watches from his jacket pocket. Since this dude was so brazen, I asked him where he had gotten them from. He said, "You don't think that I'm that stupid, do you?" When we arrived at his destination, he asked would I be willing to accept one of these watches for the ride. I said, "Sure," looked through the lot and selected one.

I was cruising in the vicinity of Harbor Place, stopped for the traffic light in the right curb lane, when I noticed two well developed white girls hitchhiking. From observation, one could sense that they hung around the red light district of the city. They asked me would I take them to Pratt and Patterson Park for nothing. I said to them, "Haven't you heard that Reagan has cut out the free lunch program?"

One asked what was I talking about? I told her to forget it, but I also said to one of them that if you give me a good show in the front seat, I'll transport the pair of you wherever you want. She said, "Solid."

I really could not believe that this chick had agreed. While driving, I asked the one up front, "What about the show?"

She then pulled up her tee shirt and revealed some of the prettiest titties ever - sticking straight out. She even pulled her pants and panties down and immediately snatched them up. After that she stated, "If you want more it will cost you $30.00 for the both of us."

I turned around to the chick in the back seat and she also teased me by showing me her tits. I was really, really tempted but to date, I've never purchased any ass and second my funds were limited.

* * *

I was cruising in the red light district of downtown Baltimore. At the Calvert Street side of the old Post Office, this scared white chick about 22 years old, with no shoes on, ran up to the taxi and requested me to please get her out of there. She got into the front seat and slid down below the window level. She asked me if I wanted to make some money. I told her that was what I was out for! I asked her how much money. She replied, "$5.00." I said, "$5.00, you must be kidding and it's obvious that you are in trouble." She stated, "Better still, I'll give you a blow job. Please just get me out of here!" She also said that she was a prostitute and that the cops were after her ass. I told her that all the cops can do is to run you off the *corners for hustling. She said that she was known and that they keep fucking with her. This chick really wasn't bad. She then asked me if anyone was following the taxi. My reply was "No."*

She asked, "How do you know?" I told her that I hadn't noticed any cop's cars in my rear view mirror. She told me to drive to a dark location somewhere up around Preston Street so that she could blow me. I drove, and parked the taxi behind the insurance building on Howard Street. After I had pulled my pants down, she requested me to put the light on so that she could see my stuff. I guess she was looking down in the head of my stuff for infection. I asked laughingly, "What's this with the lights, candid camera or something?" She laughed and commenced to give me a blow job. While blowing me, she stopped and asked me not to come in her mouth. I said to myself, what kind of prostitute is this; hoping that she didn't make this request to her paying customers.

Afterwards, she wanted to be transported back to the vicinity of the Block to search for her shoes. At the corner of Guilford Avenue and Baltimore Street, two tricks approached the taxi and told her that the cops had two bench warrants on her for failure to appear in court. Her reply was, "Fuck."

The chick was still looking for her shoes. I told her that I had to make some money. She asked me what was she going to do without her shoes. I replied, "I really don't know, but you are going to have to get the fuck out of here!"

Patrons, motorists, and pedestrians ask cabbies many questions concerning where they can acquire whatever they are looking for and will become upset if you do not have an answer. Directions of the entire city is a biggie; second where can they purchase a bag of weed (marijuana), third what is a good restaurant, and finally they ask for reasonable and decent hotel accommodations. Some out-of-town motorists will even pay the meter fare to get where they are going and follow you in their vehicle. Many cabbies like to expound upon their knowledge of the city that they represent.

Different races and age groups have various names for cab operators. Young black males will call the cabbie and their friends either "Yoe" or "Moe." The meanings of those names are unknown, but they are of ethnic origin and considered uncomplimentary. The older blacks and whites, (let's say of the middle class) will refer to you as "Mack." The elderly poor whites may sometimes refer to you as "boy." Women and the sophisticated will refer to you as "driver" or "cabbie." An apartment doorman will also make reference to you as "cabbie."

The average cabbie drives between 150 to 200 miles during a twelve hour shift. His confinements are within the city boundaries and he can only go out of the city limits if a fare's destination is beyond them. City cabs are only permitted to pick up a county fare when he returns for an individual fare that he has transported to a specific county location. A cabbie drives over his path numerous times during a shift and notices a lot of people and things about people when he is for hire.

Downtown is like the hub of a wheel with its main arteries serving as spokes leading directly to all sections of town. While driving an empty cab in the downtown area, a driver cannot help but notice the number of derelicts, both men and women, otherwise known as "shopping bag people" who search through public trash cans for food, cigarettes, clothing, and other useful items. Whatever they find that may be of use later will be placed in their shopping bags. Some will pace back and forth like a dog in front of a public trash can or eating establishment, looking for food or waiting to be fed. There is a religious place downtown that feeds them daily. At night, during the winter months, these people are seen cuddled up in vestibules of store fronts to protect themselves from the elements. These shopping bag people are from all walks of life; various defeats have contributed to their drop out or peasant behavior. It appears that most of them could never return to a realistic or normal life style.

Many times after people are seated they will ask you to give them a good number for tonight. I often reply that they all are good from 000-999. They will look at your badge number, cab number, and zero in on various tag numbers as we travel the streets. Many will state how they just missed hitting the number by being a digit off, and others will talk of their pet number hitting on a given day that they did not play. Some will tell the biggest lies concerning how often they hit and the big monies they have made off the lottery. People from all races and economic groups play the Maryland State Lottery. The lottery is big business in this city, especially with the poor!

> Transported a fare to the 200 block of North Milton Avenue. After the fare was paid, I continued south and was attempting to make a right turn on to Baltimore Street when I noticed a group of white teenagers standing on the corner. One yelled, "Hey nigger," then mooned me with his white ass. It was really funny; I just laughed and continued my turn on to Baltimore Street.

From my point of view as a hack operator, **the basics in life appear to be sex, power, money, drugs, and rock & roll.** These categories are the topics of most of my patrons' discussions. We all have money, just that some have so much more than others. **"Money and environment molds us into whatever we are."** Somewhat legitimately earned money can contribute to one being decent stock and having values. Dirty money or making fast money will not change a person's values. Many people always complain that money would be the cure to their problems. If they had it in abundance, many would not know what to do with it. Money will change some, and others it will not do a damn thing for.

> This white nurse about 25 years old hailed me in front of a local hospital in East Baltimore. She stated that she wanted to go somewhere in the Charles Village area. En route the lady started talking and revealed that she was pregnant. The lady wasn't showing, but she was congratulated! She revealed that she didn't want to be congratulated and the only reason that she was having the child was for the "Money." My reply was, **"FOR WHAT?** What money are you talking about?"
>
> Replying that she was single and hated children with a passion but she wanted to experience a pregnancy. With that in mind, the lady searched for a mate from good stock and high intelligence. She stated that after the child was born, she would sell it to the highest bidder, not accepting anything less than ten thousand dollars. I

asked, "Where are your morals, and what will your mother and family think?"

"Fuck what my mother thinks. Besides I have not seen her for ten years." The lady stated that she had it all planned and after the baby was born it would go on the black market in Florida. The lady said that in comparison it is essentially the same thing that adopting agencies do - **only difference is that she is reaping all of the benefits.** *Then she said that there would be no red-tape for the prospective parents. After the lady paid her fare and exited the cab, I said to myself,* **"There are many, many women around who would want to have and rear their own child, and here is this woman who wants to bear a child for the experience and the money only."** *That's heavy; it takes all kinds to make a world.*

* * *

I picked up this well dressed black family, husband, wife, and daughter, at North and Charles. The husband asked me to take him to a street up in Waverly, but first he wanted to circle the vicinity of North and Charles several times. He told me that he was looking for an accident that was supposed to have occurred at that intersection. An ambulance and a police car were also on the scene.

After circling the block for about ten minutes and finding nothing, he asked me to take them home. He told me that once he got home, he was going to tune in his "CB" and find out the exact location of the accident.

Next, the man asked me for a cigarette. I don't smoke but I gave him one out of a pack that someone had left in the cab. The man pulled out a roll that must have been four inches thick and asked if he could buy the remainder of the pack from me. "Sure for a buck," I said. He gave me the buck for the cigarettes and I thought to myself that I'd never seen a money roll that thick before in my life. Thinking they were probably all ones with a twenty dollar bill facing. The man once again became disgusted over the fact that he didn't find an accident at North and Charles. So I asked him if someone in his family was *involved and why was he so upset. He told me that he was an ambulance chaser. For a very handsome piece of money, he and his family would testify or swear before an attorney and/or insurance investigation that they had witnessed the accident and that the other people were totally **WRONG** concerning motor vehicle laws. I said to myself, "Boy people are a trip, and to top it off they are poisoning their teenaged daughter's mind with this type of corrupt shit."*

Sex appears to be a problem with both males and females. Many just do not seem to be getting any. Some men appear to be dogs the way they holler out of the cab windows at strange women. At times, it appears through their stares at women on the streets that they are visualizing a sexual relationship. The women are just as bad as the men, but only in a more subtle way. They will talk of loneliness and how satisfying it would be to have a real man. Even married people are unhappy and talk of a good wholesome relationship. The sexes cause a lot of problems for each other and they always will, because most experiences in life seem to revolve around sex.

A fare got out at 25th and Charles Streets and another one got in at the same location. He stated that he wanted to go to the Orchard Homes located in the vicinity of Biddle and Pennsylvania Avenue. From the dude's conversation, he came off as a fag. He started asking me some very deep questions about my personal life.

While en route to his destination, he requested that I stop at the liquor store at Park and McMechen so that he could purchase some beer. When he returned to the vehicle, we once again got involved in a conversation about life and its problems. He then asked me if I were gay. My reply was, "Do I look as if I am supposed to be?" He gave me some type of an answer. He then offered me a beer.

When I arrived at his destination, he asked me to come into his apartment. My reply was "No thanks."

The fag paid his fare and placed his hand on my knee. I advised him not to do that again. He once again put his hand on my knee. At this point, I took my fist and hit him as hard as I could in the chest. He rocked back and told me that it didn't hurt and that if and when I got horny, to look him up. I said, "Man you are disgusting; just get the fuck out of here before I have to drag you out."

* * *

I was traveling south on Cathedral Street. At the intersection of Monument, I was hailed by these two white fags and a female. I had a fare and I asked if it was okay. He replied, "Man do what you have to do to make that buck." They stated that they wanted to go somewhere in South Baltimore.
One brazen fag seated in the rear leaned up on the seat and started looking at the hair on my arms and chest. He then stated to the other fag that I had a nice basket, referring to my pelvic area. The fag then asked me if I would like to go to this party in South Baltimore. I told him that I would have to think about it! He stated that, "If you don't want to fuck with us then the chick in the middle will blow you."
I said, "All right!"
My original fare got out at Trailways Bus Station. Once he exited these people really carried on. Their whole conversation was about every conceivable sex act in the book. When I arrived at their destination, I decided to go into the party. I really wanted to see how these white fags partied!
The house was absolutely beautiful. A spiral staircase was located in the center of the house. The walls of the interior were painted white-white. The floors were covered with a heavy thick wall-to-wall carpet. The house appeared to have been one of those one dollar houses that had been restored with a modern touch. It appeared that whoever decorated the house loved space. I guess there were about fifteen gay men and two straight women. I was the only black person there. These people were real classy and sophisticated gays. They were not like common, street, exhibitionist-type fags that I had

encountered as a vice cop and cab driver. These men were really girlish acting; they greeted each other by kissing one another in the mouth. From my conversation and observation of some of the fags, they all appeared to be professional people. One told me that he was employed as a third grade elementary school teacher. Others were employed in other professions that macho or more masculine men would not care to hold. I talked to one of them and he explained how this had become his way of life. He said, "I tried women, even lived with one, but it just wasn't for me. Whenever I was intimate with a woman I got sick to my stomach. I became violently ill. I knew then that it was not for me."

"How long have you known this?" I asked.

"I understood it thoroughly and accepted it about a year ago."

We got to talking to one of the chicks and she told me that she liked to party with gays and that they were so much fun. No drugs were in sight, and they had all the refreshments and whiskey around that one could imagine or want.

I respected the actions of these people. They appeared relaxed in doing what they wanted to do in life! The one that had invited me was breathing on me like I was going to be his trick for the evening. Everywhere I turned, he was there. I asked the owner of the house, where the bathroom was. He informed me that it was up the spiral staircase. I really wanted to see the upstairs of this house and to see if this creep was eventually going to follow me. Upstairs was very nice, consisting of a music room and a well decorated bedroom. When I entered the bathroom, I purposely didn't lock the door. My instinct was right, while peeing, the creep came busting into the bathroom. I informed him that if I were a gay or fag lover that I would never have a desire for him as strong as he came on! All the time I was talking, he was attempting to look at my dick! I put my shit away, washed my hands, and went back downstairs. I thanked the host for his hospitality and explained to him that I had to return to work. On my way out, I noticed the other creep (about 35-years-old) who was in the taxi appeared to be the life of the party. But after looking at him, he was really lonely. As I was leaving, he asked to come out to Catonsville and have a nude swim. I told him that I was sorry but I'd have to pass. All in all, it was an interesting experience. It had contributed to my learning that gays are people and that they have feelings too.

* * *

Bidded on a call in the vicinity of Chester and Orleans Streets. I was dispatched to the 3500 block of Orleans Street. These two ladies dressed like prostitutes entered the taxi. They stated that they wanted to go to a used car lot on Harford Road. While driving, I heard one chick state, "Mama, something . . ." After hearing that, I attempted to make them feel good by stating, "If you are mother and daughter, you certainly look good!"
They replied together, "Why thank you."
Then the lady who was the mother stated that she had purchased a car three weeks ago and had been having nothing but trouble with it. She also revealed that the car had been in the shop four times within the past three weeks. She said, "I finally had to get a lawyer, because that bastard started giving me a lot of shit." Then she added, "This car shit is fucking with my pocketbook."
The daughter then stated that she could have made an easy three hundred dollars last weekend. I became curious and asked these two hillbilly looking women where did they work. They stated, "What the hell, we are hookers."
I told them that I had never known of a mother-daughter prostitute team before. The daughter stated, "Sure, we have been doing it for years." I told them that I had read about it, "but I've never witnessed it." They told me that they go out to truck stops and fuck the truckers. They revealed that many times they fuck right in the cabs of the trucks. "Those mother-truckers sure don't mind spending big paper," the mother stated.

"I guess they don't." I replied.
At the dealership, the mother paid the fare and gave me a nice tip. Watching them walk away from the taxi, I couldn't imagine who would want the pair of them. The old saying goes,"There is someone for everyone." The mother was a pig weighing about one hundred and seventy five pounds and the daughter was a piglette running a close second.

* * *

I was cruising in the 1100 block of Cathedral Street when hailed by this elderly white gentleman who later revealed that he was coming from the Waxter Center. He hobbled to the taxi and requested me to take him to the senior citizen place located in the vicinity of the Inner Harbor. Once the man was seated in the cab, I remembered chauffeuring him before. He then asked did I work at night and how were the ladies in the area of the Block.
He kept inquiring about the ladies of the street, I told him, "If you want a woman, it will cost you fifty dollars, plus a nice tip for me."
I really didn't have any ladies; I just wanted to see where this old-assed-man was coming from.
"I really don't have fifty dollars, but I am willing to pay twenty bucks," the old man stated.
"Ha ha ha. You couldn't even get one of the street walkers during these inflationary times for twenty bucks."
"Could you get me a black or a white chick?"
"If the money is right, I'll get you whatever you want."
"Well, what I'm really looking for is something a little steady that I can take out to a show and have dinner with."
"After dinner," he continued, "I would eat her, then I would want her to give me a little head."
"You sure want an awful lot for twenty bucks." When he exited from the taxi, he told me to keep him in mind, and, "One day, I just might have that fifty bucks." "OK, I said, but for what you want from a chick, I think you will have to have considerably more than fifty dollars"

After observing this old man hobbling out of the taxi I really believed that a "good nut" would kill him. However, I also believe that he would enjoy expiring at precisely that moment that he finally got over the brink one more time. That final sexual relationship to him would be all the proof that he needed that he once lived.

We definitely live in a drug oriented society. Practically every person under thirty indulges, and many over thirty have indulged. It is the focal issue of all races and economic status groups. **The types of drugs used run the gauntlet from amphetamines to barbiturates, heroin to cocaine, and hashish to marijuana.** Usage includes your most aristocratic to the poorest man in the ghetto. Junkies are transported in cabs around town in search of a fix. On more than one occasion, deals have gone down directly in my view, and I am sure in the view of other cabbies. Transactions can take place in the front of the taxi, or they may take place in the rear seat of the taxi. Either way, the users and the dealers conduct their business in full view of the cabbie, and they are not in the least bit concerned that the cabbie knows. Junkie patrons have been transported to doctor's offices to obtain a prescription for their habits. A lot of people of importance are involved in the use and distribution of illegal narcotics. It is sad but true, the situation is very widespread. **It is totally out of control.**

Bidded on a call in the 500 block of West Lafayette Avenue. When I arrived at the location, I observed this wheelchair dude in the vestibule waiting for me. I had to exit the cab and help the dude to the vehicle. Once the dude was seated, he stated that he was in search of some dope. He instructed me to drive in the area of 24th and Barclay. While driving, he said that his long stay in the hospital and confinement to that chair turned him into a dope addict. This dude was about forty. My reply to his comments as to why he was an addict was "Yeah, sure."

I must have driven around the vicinity of 24th and Barclay ten times so that this dude could find someone holding heroin. The dude appeared real desperate and could not score anywhere. At the intersection of North and St. Paul, he spotted a friend of his who was also a junkie. The dude called to him, asking if he knew where he could score. He stated that some guy may have some "shit" in the 2200 block of Greenmount Avenue. The dude in the cab told the other guy to get in and if he scored, they could fire together. These men were the oldest junkies that I had ever seen. They were, or at least looked to be approaching fifty years of age. **I was always under the impression that junkies died off by the time they reached forty.**

In the 2200 block of Greenmount Avenue, they could not find a supplier, so, I was instructed to drive to Lexington and Fremont Streets. While en route to that location, these dudes really got into the junkie jargon and some personal talk. The wheel chair dude was explaining to his friend that he had gotten shot over a woman who was sleeping around. He caught her head up with a guy. He and the other guy pulled pistols and he got the worst of it.

At the intersection of Lexington and Fremont Streets, the other dude got out and started asking around about who was holding. Lexington and Fremont Streets are considered to be located in the inner city which contains low income and high rise projects. The dude gets back into the cab and revealed that the junk man on Fayette was holding.

I was instructed to drive to the intersection of Fayette and Fremont Streets. At this location, the wheelchair dude gave the other guy $75.00 after he requested it. The dude took the money, approached and gave it to the junk man who appeared to be about 50 years-old. The junk man took the money and disappeared in a vacant building on Fayette Street. He returned and gave the guy something. The wheelchair dude and I could see that he had scored. The guy got back into the cab, stated, "That was Blue, who had been dealing in junk for a long time." After the guy was seated, both of them inspected the package which was in a brown envelope. I was curious and really wanted to see what this dude had paid his $75.00 for, but I kept my eyes forward and pretended to concentrate on my driving. I overheard the guy tell the wheelchair dude that *he was damn glad that he called him over to the cab and that he had not had any stuff for a good while. The way these guys were talking, I thought they were going to fire up in the cab, but then I heard the wheelchair dude reveal that he had his works in his room at his mother's house. I transported them back to Lafayette Avenue. The wheelchair dude gave me $15.00 and thanked me for being so patient.*

My thoughts, after they had departed were that it is quite expensive being a junkie, cab fares and the money spent for the stuff. That is some life one has to live dealing with that shit! I feel kind of sorry for hard core junkies.

* * *

Picked up this white man at 25th and Charles Streets who appeared to be about 40 years old. He stated that he wanted to be transported to Baltimore Street and Guilford Avenue.

En route to that location, he started talking about how good he was feeling because he had just kicked the heroin habit by locking himself in a room for the last six days. He revealed that he had been using drugs for the last 23 years. The habit cost him and his girlfriend about $200 a day. He stated that she sells pussy so that they can stay high.

He told me that his lady ran out on him about a week ago and left him with their small child. He told me that the child was with him while he was withdrawing. He stated that if the mother didn't return soon, he was going to file a missing persons report. He revealed that his lady's habit cost them about $70,000 a year. He stated that they really could have lived well for $70,000. He said that he would steal anything to keep his habit going. For the last ten minutes, this guy had been telling how he had kicked his heroin habit.

He now revealed that he was going downtown to get a small bag of heroin, so that he could get his stomach together. I asked if that wouldn't defeat what he had been trying to do for the last six days. He said, "No, that one *bag will not make me a junkie." My reply was **"Oh yeah," saying to myself, who are you fooling.** He then talked about how he had to go downtown in a taxi to get his shit and that the nigger that he scores from rides around in a big Cadillac. He also revealed that he didn't have any money to score but that getting the stuff from this dude would not be a problem. He told me that the source knows that once you pick your habit up, you will return to stealing. What the junkie was saying was that it was to the source's advantage to give him a free bag of heroin.*

Some of the best "hustlers" in town will hang around the bus stations. Before a bus patron leaves the station, he could be hustled by a hack, prostitute, pimp, or cabbie. These people hang in and around the station. Hackers and cabbies will try to make deals relative to transporting to various locations in the metropolitan area. Prostitutes and fags will hang in the general vicinity looking for a trick. Pimps are there in search of runaways or confused females. At one of the bus stations, there is even a dude that hustles cabs for patrons and expects a tip from the cab rider and the cabbie. People who hang around bus stations are some of your best schemers or stick-up artists in the world.

There is a difference between night and day in the downtown city life! During the daytime, the streets of downtown are filled with professional people - secretaries, clerks, and office workers. Basically white collar and blue collar employees, but at night, the tempo changes and parts of downtown become "red light districts".

In the vicinity of the old Post office building at Fayette and Guilford and Baltimore and Guilford Streets, fags dressed as drag queens and prostitutes approach motorists and pedestrians relative to their trade. Some will hang over mailboxes and make gestures to passersby. Some of the drag queens outshine the hookers with their revealing dress and "silicon titties."

During the night, the prostitutes and drag queens sit right up in the coffee shop window located at Baltimore and Guilford making waves to motorists and pedestrians. Many of the people who go down there in search of a little play know exactly what they are getting into. Some are regular customers. The night walkers sit on downtown bus benches with their legs crossed, wearing very revealing clothing in a suggestive manner. Night walkers are also found in the 2000-2200 blocks of Pennsylvania Avenue, 2000 block of Eutaw Place, Broadway and Eastern Avenue and Fells Point, and also in the vicinity of Biddle and St. Paul Streets. At night, fags will walk around blocks of Park Avenue and Cathedral Street while hailing and making lewd gestures to motorists. Mt. Vernon Square appears to be a meeting place for fags at night.

I was cruising south in the 800 block of Cathedral Street which is known as the Mt. Vernon section of the city when hailed by a white man about 25 years old. He was standing at the bus stop. At first I didn't know if he was hitchhiking, waiting for the bus, or hailing for a cab. I stopped, just as a bus was approaching, but he instructed me to wait until he had checked with the destination of the bus. Apparently it was not the right bus because he waved it goodbye, opened the cab's door and took a seat. Once seated, he stated that he wanted to go in the vicinity of Washington Boulevard and Caton Avenue. While riding, I could feel the dude glancing at me continuously with what appeared to be fag desires through his bedroom eyes. About halfway en route, he asked did I get high and would I like to smoke a joint with him. I replied that I smoke occasionally but that I would have to pass. There was silence for awhile but the fag kept starring at me off and on. I later broke the silence and said that I would take the joint as a tip. He said that he would share one with me but that he wasn't going to give me a joint or anything in access of the fare. I said, "Solid" revealing to him, **"If I smoke a joint with you then you will want to do something else."**

He said, "Yeah, I'd like to suck your dick." My reply was "Yeah I know, and that's why I am not smoking with you." He appeared a little heartbroken after that statement. After that, our conversation appeared general. He said that he had just returned to Baltimore from New York and was presently going to visit his mother and son, after being away for some two years. From his actions, he

appeared to be quite nervous as we approached his destination. I asked 'What's wrong?"
He said that he didn't know how his mother and son were going to accept him after being away for such a long period of time. I then asked, "Does your son know or accept you as a homosexual?" He evaded the question and immediately changed the subject, and once again started talking about how he would like to get into me. I interrupted and said that you changed the subject and did not answer my question. He said that he didn't know the answer and that thinking about that "shit" was upsetting him. After paying his fare, he said, "Good night, good-looking."

Unemployment is high in this city, especially among blacks! Day after day black males are found grouped on corners in all sections of the city drinking their lives away, waiting for something to happen. Some are into drugs and others are drug dealers. It is not all their fault what has happened to them in life, but for those who exist and do nothing constructive, it is their fault that they let society mold them into this way of life. They appear to be more of a threat to themselves than to others. It is time for them to react to their crisis in life.

Many people are born, live and die within a one mile radius. They have been nowhere, and they know absolutely nothing about the city or anything else. People who have lived here all of their lives have never been to Druid Hill Park, Memorial Stadium, the Inner Harbor, nor Fort McHenry. From their conversation while they are being transported, one would think that they are in a foreign country. Some will even tell you that they never leave their neighborhoods. Many people express a dying desire to go to the Harbor. Some people, or at least the uneducated ones, think that the Harbor is off-limits to them. A lack of exposure in an environment can contribute to a poorly developed mind.

Some people have fear concerning the taxi meter. Some would rather make a bargain before permitting the operator to throw the flag; they just do not like being timed for the fare. The jumping of the meter probably makes them nervous. It is like watching money jump right out of their pockets. Some of those who are transported under the control of the meter will give you all kinds of directions, attempting to duck traffic lights, and they will have you traveling all kinds of dangerous side streets. Once they have reached their destination, they will, in a voice bordering on panic, command the operator to turn the meter off immediately. They then pay the fare and jump from the taxi.

This black lady about forty five years old flagged me in the 700 block of East Belvedere. She revealed that she wanted to go to the bank at Park Heights and Wylie. It was later revealed through our conversation that this lady was one of those "Jesus freaks." That's all she talked about all the way across town. ***Every subject that she expounded upon, the Lord was related in one way or another.*** *She told me that she was a healer and that money was basically meaningless to her. Then the woman stated that people paid her big money for her services. I asked her, "If money is meaningless, then why are you taking it for the great power that you are supposed to possess?" She clarified that by stating that people reward her with gifts.*

The woman then got into my case about not attending church - asking me to please attend her church one Sunday. My reply was that I'll try. As we approached the bank, the Jesus freak said, "Oh God, the bank looks as if it has closed and they are supposed to be open until 3:00 p.m."

I said, "Come on lady, don't give me any shit. I know you weren't depending on the bank being opened concerning my money." The lady said, "Lord, please help me."

I said, "Come off it Miss, you're nothing but a con artist. You told me that money is meaningless and that your Lord gets you anything." I said, "See if your Lord bails you out of this when the cops come."

She said, "Please Sir, don't call the cops,"

Then she showed me this filthy looking check that she pulled from her pocket. The fare was $4.00 and I asked the lady, just how much do you have? She pulled about $1.25 from her pocket. I said, "Look if I decide to let you go, when can I get my money." She said nervously, "The

bank opens back up at 5:00 p.m. stop pass my house where you picked me up and I will give you the balance."
I said, "All right lady."
She God blessed me, thanked me for not calling the cops, and got out of the cab. I got my money, but it took about a week to catch up with this lady.

* * *

This guy from Tokyo flagged me at the intersection of Harford Road and North Avenue. It was obvious that he had just left Sears because he had a crated color television set in his possession. He instructed me to drive him to St. Paul and 33rd Streets. We started talking and I learned that he was an exchange student at Johns Hopkins and would be in this country approximately one year. He also stated that he had been in the States for a week and finds them very interesting. He revealed that it is very, very expensive to live in this country. My reply was, "Yeah tell me about it."
He revealed that the fare from Tokyo to the States was $1,000. I told him that I have a great desire to go to Europe and Japan. At his destination, he asked me how much was the fare and I advised him that it was $2.50. He stated that he couldn't get used to what is known as tipping in this country. Revealed that in Tokyo or Japan there is no such thing as tipping, anywhere. I found that to be very interesting. He gave me 50 cents in excess of the meter fare and asked was that acceptable. My reply was that, "I wish that every passenger would give me a 50¢ tip."

* * *

This elderly man motioned for me at Pennsylvania and Laurens. It took him a while to get over and into the taxi. Once he was situated, he stated that he wanted to go to the food stamp place on the Avenue. Well, I picked the man up at Pennsylvania and Laurens and the food stamp place is located about 75 yards north on Pennsylvania Avenue. I said to myself that this is the shortest cab ride *that I had ever transported a person for hire. At the food stamp place, I told the man that the fare was $1.10. The man stated that he was a poor man and that I was robbing him. I told him that I had no idea where he was going and that I had no control over the meter. He searched through his pockets and gave me four quarters and a dime. While exiting the taxi, the man put a curse on me, stating that "Jesus will get even with you for cheating an old man". I told him to have a nice day and please don't do that to me.*

Ethnic groups live in clusters throughout the city. Sections of Northwood, Govans, Waverly, Irvington and a few other areas have housed blacks for years, but were traditionally white. Ethnic grouping and living is a part of Baltimore City's heritage and will probably remain that way forever.

Baltimore can be difficult to get around because of its named streets. To know this city, one has to take time and learn it. Apart from Baltimore being divided by ethnic groups and having different neighborhoods, the city is also divided geographically into north, south, east, and west sections. The east/west boundary line is Charles Street which runs north to south. Charles Street has culture and class. Starting from South Charles going north you find row houses and a commercial shopping area called Mount Vernon which contains historical buildings, monuments, restaurants, clubs, and a bohemian style of living. Then there is Charles Village which would be classified as residential /bohemian/commercial. Next is the college district with Johns Hopkins University, some luxury high rise apartment buildings and Loyola College. Finally, the Charles Street high rent district which extends well out into Baltimore County.

The north/south boundary is Baltimore Street which runs east to west. Baltimore Street does not possess the same qualities as Charles Street. Baltimore Street outside the downtown area is somewhat of an imaginary race boundary line between ethnic groups with many being of the same social economic status. Blacks live to the north and whites to the south of Baltimore Street. Sometimes problems do occur with some of these people as they shop and socialize in the commercial districts of Baltimore Street.

Baltimore Street east and west outside the downtown area presents a blue collar or low income lifestyle.

The senior citizen housing program works well in this city, especially for those in need. The high rise developments are geographically located in every neighborhood of the city. The developments are no more than ten years old. Some industrial factories and old school buildings have been converted into apartment units for this program. The high rise units are secure and a blessing to many of the elderly and disabled. Baltimore has to be a leader in the country with its senior citizen housing program.

I was driving south on Howard Street when hailed by this individual at Preston Street who later revealed himself to be a senior citizen. After he entered the cab, he made a deal with me to take him to this bingo joint in the Brooklyn section of the city for $5.00.

En route, we passed this high rise located on Park Avenue in the vicinity of the Greyhound Bus Station. He stated, "That place houses every type of individual one could conceivably think of," referring to blacks, whites, prostitutes, homosexuals, cripples, and the elderly. I then asked him how did he know this. He revealed that he used to be a guard there. Then the man started talking about the place where he lives. As he started, I asked where was the place located. He said in the vicinity of the Fifth Regiment Armory. He told me that some people will take advantage of you until the day you die. I asked him what was he talking about? He stated that most of his building was black, and most of these blacks received checks during the first week of the month and do not have checking or savings accounts. The building has a Jewish male and a black female senior citizen team who charge the disabled a minimum of $10.00 to cash their checks. He stated that the Jewish man would make deposits and withdrawals all at the same time so that he would have available cash.

Revealing that the team was making about $600.00 a month from these people. I told him that was not a bad piece of tax free money! He then revealed that they would charge people for everything. If they went shopping for *groceries for any senior citizen, a percentage would be deducted from the tenant's money for their troubles. The man stated that he did not have a dime but he did not condone this type of "Bullshit."*

He further stated that the team got mad with him because he advised the people to deposit their checks directly into a bank of their choice. He also told those who were unable to get accounts to use the services of the food markets. He also stated that cashing checks in the markets could be bad business because the muggers are milling about in the vicinities during check week for women, the poor, and the elderly.

I said, **"Life is a bitch, ain't it?"**

After talking to this senior citizen, I could understand his concern, but in reality, the team was not doing anything illegal. I think that they were a bit overpaid for the services rendered and that they were taking advantage of the helpless and the ignorant. Really, I think that this has something to do with a person's morals! I believe that what goes around comes around!

* * *

I was cruising west on East North Avenue when hailed by this elderly black lady at the intersection of Wolfe Street. She told me to take her to Warwick and Edmondson Avenues. Once the lady was comfortable, she revealed that her church was having revival all that week. She stated that she has been feeling excellent since attending. Then the lady asked me if I attended church and what was my religion. I told her that I really didn't attend church and that I was reared as a Catholic. I then told her that I do have faith! She asked me when was the last time that I was actually in a church. I told her that I guess that I went twice last year. She said, "You ought to be ashamed but at least you've been in a house of worship recently."

All the while this lady was pumping and preaching to me, she kept a mindful eye on the meter. When she entered the cab, she named her route, and was well aware of what the fare should run. The lady started talking about Communion Sunday in her church. She also said that some ladies feel so happy on Communion Sunday that when they go to the altar, they leave their pocketbooks behind in the pews. Revealed that a couple of her girlfriends have returned to the pews finding out that their pocket- books had been rifled. My reply was, "Really, I didn't believe that anything like that would happen in a place of worship."

The lady revealed that when she goes to Communion, she carries her pocketbook with her, and when she kneels in front of the altar, one knee is placed upon it. I told her that I never heard of such in a place of worship.

At her destination, the meter read $5.40 or something like that. She gave me a $10.00 bill - I gave her the silver change and she got out the cab. As the woman started to walk away, I stated, "Miss I owe you four additional dollars."

She stated "Oh, thank you and God bless you for being so honest." She gave me a quarter tip and some church literature. I felt like saying that I really don't have to attend church to have morals!

* * *

I was cruising in the vicinity of Baltimore and Charles Streets when hailed by three white males in the unit block of East Baltimore Street. Once they were seated in the taxi the one up front told me to take them to Loch Raven and Northern Parkway. En route, the guy up front asked me, "Would you believe that fool in the backseat jumped in the harbor in front of the Pratt Street Pavilion for $5.00?" The guy who jumped in the harbor interjected by stating, "You goddamn right!" and that he would do it any day of the week for $5.00. He told me that he was in the Navy and that he didn't make $5.00 an hour, more or less a minute. The man up front started teasing him about the sliminess of the dirty harbor water. It was really funny looking at the guy who jumped in the harbor and smelling the odor from the dried clothes.

Hey Cabbie

Tourists and Baltimoreans will talk of the changes in the city within the last ten years and express how they like the new Baltimore. They will talk about how the Mayor and developers have done such a great job with the downtown area and the Inner Harbor. They love the combination of the old as well as the new architectural structures. They also like the purple/green/white directories the city has geographically placed around the city for guidance.

Baltimore is a progressive town! Everything one wants to find is around here somewhere. At times you may have to look harder than in other cities. One can find the arts, sports, entertainment, cultural living, and recreation. As far as being involved with "who is who", one has to be involved in more or less a social "clique."

The city is backward in many ways. Some people cannot read or write at all and many no not know the city beyond their own neighborhoods. Directions are definitely out. As a cabbie, one has to interpret within his own mind what these people are saying and actually figure out where they are going. It is amazing, but through trial and error, you manage to get them to their destination. Some of these people can literally kill the King's English!

Had this job in the taxi traveling west of Fayette Street, when hailed by this black gentleman at the intersection of Fayette and Eutaw Streets. First, he stated that he wanted to go to Mount Royal Terrace and McCulloh Street. I said, "Come again, the streets run parallel."

He said "I am sorry, I mean North and McCulloh". After he got comfortable in the taxi, he started talking about his losings at the track. He remarked, now that he had lost his money, he was going home, change his clothes, and go visit his sister in Northwood.

He then asked me would I return to the 2400 block of McCulloh Street and take him to Northwood after I dropped the lady off in the backseat. I let the man off and continued on to the vicinity of Druid Hill Park where the lady wanted to go. Then I returned to the 2400 block of McCulloh Street and blew the horn for the man. He entered the taxi, stating that he wanted to go to the 1800 block of Belvedere.

He then asked would I like a drink. I replied, "Don't mind if I do". We stopped pass the drugstore located in the 2500 block of Eutaw Place. He returned with a pint of rum and a coke. He stated that "They did not have any cups, and I hope that you do not eat pussy." My reply was "Hell no man."

After we had a couple of hits out the bottle, the man opened up and started talking. First he stated that he was from some place in Virginia; he had to quit school in the third grade to work the farm and support his family. He revealed that he had seven sisters and that he contributed to sending them to school. He went on to say that after his parents died, his sisters did him kind of dirty by taking family heirlooms that should have been rightfully his.

This guy was a real neat individual, clear skin, hair well kept, and he did not smell like others that I sometimes encounter. (If you work with the public, you know what I am talking about). He revealed that he was fifty years old. The man appeared wholesome and sincere. He talked very well, basically no bad English. Then the man told me that he could not read a lick. I then asked, "Would you know the difference between a street sign that read Belvedere Avenue or Northern Parkway". He stated, "No". I said, "You telling me that you do not know the alphabet"? His reply was that he did not know the alphabet or what the letters meant. This was so hard for me to believe that this man had been robbed for fifty years of his life simply because he could not read. He said that the only way that he knew his way around was through various landmarks. This guy had to have had a difficult time in life, constantly faking his way through.

He told me that he was employed as a truck driver. I asked him how did he make it from one place to another. He said, "I manage." He said that his sisters were trying to persuade him to go to night school. He said that he was too old. I told him, "You are never too old to learn." He replied, "That's what my sisters have been telling me." The man was really revealing that he was embarrassed about his deficiency. He told me that Calvert Adult

Hey Cabbie

Educational Center had a program for adult non-readers. I said, "You really shouldn't feel embarrassed about this. You should go ahead and sign up. If they have such a program at the center, then there must be others who have the same problem."

I could not understand how this guy could go to the race track, bet on horses, and not be able to read a lick. If you looked at and talked to this guy, you just would not believe it. I guess Baltimore has many functional illiterates.

Today people are very polite concerning smoking in an enclosed place. Before lighting up a cigarette, they will ask permission. Many people need this vice while relaxing to relieve their tensions and frustrations they encountered during the course of their day. Stopping them from smoking after they have hired your services could put a damper on the tip. Some patrons, after opening the door, will stand outside and ask if it is okay to smoke in the taxi. If you say no, some will slam the door and look for another means of transportation. To some riders, smoking is very important.

People wear their environment! Their odors tell a lot about their character, personality and background. Some of the smells a cabbie has to tolerate from patrons are bad breath, body odor, foul house odors, what they had for dinner odors and occupational odors. Many times these smells are embedded in their clothes. At times you have to put up with the smell of some women who are on their menstrual cycle - or at least I think that's what it is. Being enclosed with some of these people and their smells can be terribly sickening. During these uncomfortable times, all the cabbie wants to do is to get them to their destination as quickly as possible before the bottom of his stomach erupts like Mount St. Helens.

At times I am often surprised at what I have to do to make a buck. I was cruising south on Broadway when hailed by this drunk at Eager Street. Someone helped him into the cab, and he stated that he wanted to go to some project court in the vicinity of Pratt and Bond Streets. The man was stinking like a sewer and he was slobbering all over himself like a rabid animal, his eyes were red and blood shot, and his mouth, nose and face looked like the ass of an estrusing baboon. Ordinarily, I do not pick these types of individuals up, but the day was extremely slow and I needed the money. When I arrived at his destination, he stated, "You got to come wid me to git ya money."

I said, "Hey man, you didn't tell me that shit when you sat your filthy ass in my cab." He looked at me with his sad red eyes and nodded. "I am not going anywhere, and you'd better get my money."

"Ok, ok, ok," he muttered. "I have to go and get it."

"Well if you have to go and get my money, I would appreciate it if you would leave something behind you which is of some value." He pulled out of his pocket this scroungy looking handkerchief and a well used wallet. He placed the two items on the front seat.

"Just what am I supposed to do with this shit?" I asked.

"Just wait one fucking minute," he replied. He then pulled off his horrible looking right shoe, reached down into his smelly sock and pulled out this sweaty-stinky ten dollar bill and handed it to me. Man I was scared to touch the thing, so I handled it by the edges. I gave the man his change and he started to walk away from the cab. I called to the man, "What about this shit you left on the front seat?" referring to his funky wallet and soiled handkerchief. He staggered back to the cab, retrieved his shit and said to me, **"You think you is a smart, cute nigger, don't you?"** *After the man got his stuff, I said, "Have a nice day." I immediately went to Hopkins Hospital and washed my hands with some surgical soap. Man, you would be surprised at the amount of germy people that I come in contact with out there.*

Since BWI Airport has been remodeled, city cabs have just about been shut out from procuring a fare to or from the airport. A cabbie has to purchase an expensive medallion from somewhere in order to sit in a BWI taxi stand. Then one has to wait on the outer perimeter of the arrival horse-shoe and hope that a fare notices him. BWI cabs work in rotation, have reserved parking in the most inner lane, and some of them will actually go into the terminal to hustle a fare. The poor city cabbie who has a BWI medallion has to stay with the cab at all times. If they break the rules, they are subject to being ticketed by the state police. Most city cabs will just transport to the BWI Airport then "deadhead" back to the city. **The taxi setup at BWI Airport is unfair and unconstitutional.**

People complain about a cabbie's driving, especially if he is driving within the speed limit. They will say or rather ask, "Are we in a wake or on a sightseeing tour of Baltimore?" Some will reveal how much of a hurry they are in and will give you the command to step on it. If you ask how much is it worth to get them there quickly, many will say nothing and some will say "Oh you are one of those kind." **Then you will have to explain to the people that you drive for a living and that the privilege can be easily taken away.**

Cab driving makes one become aware of society. **If one is perceptive, he sees just about everything for what it is worth ... No matter where you go or where you are, PEOPLE ARE PEOPLE!** We have the same habits of life. From this industry, one can see that we are really animals. We work, and we are rewarded with money. We are trained and conditioned animals, much like Pavlov's dog. The money we receive is basically used for the essentials of life, food, shelter and clothing. What little that is left over is used for entertainment and incidental living. **A handful of people make decisions and will guide us through our lives. The rest of us are just followers. The decision makers have our lives programmed until someone stands up and rebels**. Rebels are generally shot or put in jail. We are governed by our inner selves, or at least attempted to be governed by some inner motivation, but the government and its agents with the slightest hint of a threat to get out of line, will take steps to insure your compliance. In this society, "man watches man," and "dog eats dog." Bureaucratic agencies maintain the status quo. We are domesticated animals to somebody or for something. There is virtually nothing short of annihilation that man can do to stop people en masse from going off. What is a secret? It is something unexplained or kept hidden from others. ...it shouldn't be shared unless confidentially with a selected few. Secrets arise from birth, sex, power, jealousy, rivalry, love, hate, death, etc. that's why they are never kept ... People share some pretty powerful secrets with cabbies. Why they do this God only knows. There is a possible explanation in that because they are in the company of a stranger, a one-on-one basis, a stranger who appears to be in charge of their destination for a brief moment in their lives, they feel confident in revealing an important part of self to the cabbie. A cabbie plays many roles out here during the course of a day, but his biggest task is being an amateur psychologist or sociologist to his fares. Hardly a day goes by in a cabbie's career that he is not confronted with his fare's problems. Many are looking for logical solutions from the cabbie's point of view. Some just want to blow off steam and use the cabbie as the lightening rod ... After people become relaxed in a cab, many will discuss their frustrations in their lives ... some of their problems are about their jobs, friends neighbors, etc. and they do not appear to be very serious. However some problems are a little more deeply rooted concerning families, loved ones, adventures, and close friends. **It is just unbelievable the confidence that people will have in a cabbie and things that they are willing to reveal...**

On a particular date, about 4:00 p.m., I was sitting in front of the Hilton Hotel at the taxi stand on Fayette Street. This black guy about 25-30 years old asked this white cab driver in front to transport him and the driver refused. The guy was real dirty and appeared high. He then approached my cab asking me to take him to York Road and Winston Avenue. He then showed me his money. After the guy was seated in the cab, he stated that he had a couple of stops to make. First, he wanted to pick up his friend at Liberty and Fayette Streets and second, a stereo set that he had just purchased in the 300 block of Liberty Street. His friend jumped in the cab in the middle of Fayette Street and this guy had in his possession a bucket of chicken and fried potatoes. He offered some to his friend riding up front and to me. I refused but his friend accepted.

While driving up Park Avenue, the guy with the chicken threw a half-pint of Vodka on to the front seat of the cab. These two dudes were really wild. After they picked up his stereo set, we continued to York Road and Winston Avenue via Calvert Street. Seeing City Jail off Fallsway and Madison Street, one of the men told me to hurry and get him pass that place. He said that this was the first time in his life that he had been out of that place longer than a year.

Then he revealed that money comes easy and that he spends it as fast as it comes. En route to York Road, he revealed how he had obtained money for a stereo and a television that he had purchased earlier. He stated that a chick hipped him to an old man who had just made a five hundred dollar withdrawal from a particular bank on York Road. The man had entered some supermarket in the vicinity. The woman had told him that the man had placed the money in an envelope and he had later put the money and the envelope into a food cart. He stated that he had approached the cart, took the envelope and ran out of the store. He revealed that while cop cars and the police helicopter were converging on the scene, he was running in the opposite direction. From the dude's conversation and actions, he had spent everything that he had stolen. He also told me that he gave the chick one hundred and fifty dollars for hipping him to the money. He then told me how he would have to hang low for a while. For the life of me, I could not understand why this dude was revealing this escapade.

* * *

I was cruising in the BLOCK, a red light district, about 10:30 p.m. and was hailed by this white man with a beard about fifty years old. After entering the cab, he asked if I knew where he could cash a check. I told him the only place that I knew of this time of night was O'Connell's Liquors on Eastern Avenue in Highlandtown. He told me to take him there.

While riding the gentleman was silent for a moment, then he said, "Guess how much that drugstore on the corner of Baltimore and Gay wanted to cash my check." "I have no idea." He then said, "Twenty-nine dollars."

I said, "Wild man, you must have a biggie!" He then said, "Twenty-nine dollars is about five percent of the *check." I said, "Damn, you must have about a $600 check."*

He then said that he doesn't know what's happening in this world! The man requested me to wait while he cashed his check. I was told to return to Baltimore and Gay as he got back into the cab. While driving, I started thinking that some people are trusting souls. Here this man doesn't know me from a hole in the wall and I know for a fact that he has $600 cash dollars in his pocket. Some cab drivers are somewhat gangsters and would have definitely rolled the man for his $600.

If they didn't do it, then they would have probably had him followed and ripped off.

The man returned to the BLOCK more than likely to throw his money away on some show girl but by the same token I don't think that he or people should be so trusting about their money to unknown individuals.

As a cabbie, it is believed that many people just have to talk to someone. When a single passenger hires your services, many will open up with some type of conversation ... except those with some emotional or attitudinal problem.

Many people in this city are lonely and have absolutely no one to talk to. Some are married, but the majority are single. They live in houses, apartments, or rooms and really lead strange isolated lifestyles. They hang in bars and get drunk regularly. Their best friends are service type people. Some even appear to be suicidal. For the most part, they appear to be withdrawn or introverted people. It appears that they have no one special in life. Their family ties have either been broken or they have gone. The fun and relaxing aspect of their lives appear to be missing. They open up when they are situated in a one-on-one situation, especially after having a few drinks. They discuss their problems with barkeepers and cabbies.

These people actually need someone to talk with. Their whole lives revolve around them and only them. I believe that many want friends or someone to share their lives with but have really forgotten how to relate. From listening to them, they always appear to have their guards up against something. As a cabbie, you learn to listen well and basically only intervene with indirect questions or statements. They have hired your services for a limited amount of time and want you to listen to their problems. They are not interested in your complaints. Many of these people are extremely uptight about some crisis in their lives which possibly led them to be introverted and lonely. **Loneliness seems to be a serious problem for many.**

Bidded on this call in the vicinity of Dolphin and McCulloh Streets. I was dispatched to 700 Homes Court which is a project in the McCulloh homes. It was impossible to drive the taxi into the court, since it was for pedestrians only. So I drove the vehicle around to the rear. At that location, this elderly black lady opened the door and signaled me to wait.

When the lady came out of the project, I noticed all these pigeons surrounding her as she walked off the step. The lady sat two shopping bags down in her walkway so that she could rest for a moment. Because of her age, I exited the taxi and helped her with her bags. Once she was inside the taxi, I asked her why were all those pigeons around her house. I said to myself, she obviously had to be feeding them. She went on to explain that she buys cracked corn down on Lexington Street for her birds but apparently the owner got the order mixed up and sold her some other type of animal food. She stated, "Whatever type of food it is, my birds just would not eat it!" She revealed that she feeds some 600 birds and they come from as far as Druid Hill Park to her house. I do not know how this woman knew where these birds came from, so I left that alone.

The lady was 92 years-old and her mind was excellent. She could do for herself and appeared chipper for her age. She told me that she lived alone and loved it. The lady went on to state that the manager was mad with her because of her birds shitting all over the place. He contacted the Health Department but they stated that she was doing nothing wrong by feeding the birds.

At the feed store, the owner exchanged the bag of food and told her that she had been mistakenly given rabbit food. He apologized for the inconvenience. After exchanging the food, we returned to her house. I asked her whether she let the pigeons in her house. She stated, "When they are injured, I mend their wings and let them stay inside until they are healed". I inquired about the droppings; she stated that she puts paper down and that they go into a cage to shit. Once we returned to her place, I looked over from her project and noticed pigeons perched on the second floor window sills of other people's apartments. I know these tenants have to be annoyed with these birds hanging around their windows. I know I would be! I assisted the lady with her bags to her front door and observed bird shit everywhere. She also had a coffee can on the front of the building for the birds to drink from. After talking to the lady, I looked at her as a lonely, but a remarkable woman. Personally, if I were the manager of the project or a resident, I would definitely be annoyed with the bird problem. However, since I am neither, more power to the bird lady.

As a cab patron, the logic of some people is that you will never see them again, so what difference does it make what they reveal. This is not always true, but cab riding people are just like that. A regular or career cabbie will again run across regular cab patrons in time. They will tell you anything and everything about their professions, habits or life styles. Some will even respond to leading questions.

I was cruising in the vicinity of North and Pennsylvania Avenues when hailed by this man. He took a seat, lit a cigarette and instructed me to transport him to Presstman and Payson Streets. En route, he started to talk about his problem, that was a biggie! He told me that he was a married man and that he was now going to meet his girlfriend of eleven years. He stated that she wanted to terminate the relationship. He also said that they had lived in close proximity of each other. They had agreed to meet halfway, walk and talk about this shit. I asked if she wanted him to divorce his wife. His reply was yes! He further informed me that he would, but to date, he had too much at stake. I said, "I know it is hard, but you can't have your cake and eat it too."

Before departing from the cab, he revealed that he loved the woman much more than he loved his wife. It appeared that tears were coming into his eyes. I wished him the best of luck as he alighted from the cab.

Some people have problems and want to hear a complete stranger's suggestion for a solution. Many know the solutions to whatever, but they will not act upon their problems until hearing advice or at least an interpretation of the problem from a neutral source. The cabbie fits this description and he is perceived to be the ideal person.

This black chick hailed me at the intersection of Fulton and Baltimore Streets. Once she was situated in the taxi, and after she had told me where she wanted to go, she asked, "How old are you?" After I had revealed my age, she commenced to tell me her story about the problems that she had been having with her man. She told me that she lived with this dude and that lately sex had been terrible with this individual.

"Last night when I went out and returned, he accused me of having sex with another man, and he called me an alcoholic."

"Well did you?" I asked.

She told me that she did not lie and she was not in the habit of lying, but she told her friend, "Maybe I did and maybe I didn't." She said that a heavy argument ensued, and that he forced her to have sex with him. She stated that she struggled all the time and that she also attempted to scream, but he put his hands over her mouth. After that ordeal, she went outside and called the cops. She told the cops that he had raped her and that she wanted him out of her apartment. She revealed that the cops waited around until he had left the premises. The cops had explained to her that she would have to obtain a warrant from the Court Commissioner at the police district in order to charge him with rape. I really don't believe that the cops believed this woman's story at the time. I explained to her that rape was a real serious charge and before she goes through with whatever, she should give this considerable thought. Then this lady started talking about the sizes of different men's dicks. She stated that once this guy was preparing to do it to her, but he had made the mistake of leaving a dim light on. She said that she had caught a glimpse of his cock which was hanging half way down his leg while flaccid. She said that she then excused herself, went into the bathroom, put her clothes on and got the hell out of there immediately. She said that she probably could have handled it, if she had not seen it. We both had a good laugh after she told me of her adventure.

Once we were at her destination, she requested that I not park in from of the house. She explained that she was going in there to get the good stuff from this guy. I asked her what was she talking about. After seeing that this guy was at home, she returned to the taxi, paid the fare, and then she revealed to me what she meant was that this guy really knew how to make a girl feel good. I couldn't believe this chick. Here she was at one moment contemplating the possibility of charging her live-in mate with rape, and she is running around fucking someone else.

* * *

Picked up this black male alcoholic at the intersection of Fulton and Edmondson Avenues. Once in the taxi, the dude stated that he wanted to be transported to Spring Grove State Hospital. Because of the man's dress and the alcohol on his breath, I asked him to show me the money before transporting. He did.

En route to the hospital, he stated that he was an alcoholic and that his job was sending him to Spring Grove for twenty-eight days to dry out. While riding, the dude asked me to stop pass the first liquor store in sight so that he could purchase a beer. He asked me if I wanted a beer and my reply was "No."

The dude got mad and stated, "You don't have to get an attitude when someone offers you something." I remarked that I was not getting an attitude, I just didn't want anything. Then I said, "If you insist, I will take a bag of chips and a beer." The dude started getting off, "First you state that you don't want anything, and now you are telling me to get you two items." I went into my change bag and gave him a quarter for the chips. The alcoholic returned with two 16 ounce cans of beer and a bag of chips. He revealed that he had to drink his beer slowly because if he didn't he would vomit. The dude told me that he drinks beer only, and that he usually swallows three quarts before he starts work in the mornings. I told him that three quarts of beer is equal to nine shots of whiskey. He got mad and stated that he was paying me to drive and not to analyze his drinking problems. Then he told me that he had worked at Sparrows Point for 20 years and got into my case for driving a taxi. I revealed that I worked at the Point as a teenager and have no desire to return. Conveyed to him that as a taxi driver, I worked harder than ever in life! Revealing that I drive 10-12 hours a day, concentrate on the radio, be cognizant of pedestrian traffic, anticipate moves of other drivers, figure out where to make money, and carry on conversations with many of my passengers. The dude changed the subject and told me that the only reason that he was going to dry out was because his job was being threatened. Once at his destination, we shook hands. I told him that only he could do it if he really wanted to!

* * *

Bidded on a call in the vicinity of Lafayette and Eutaw. I was dispatched to the 1200 block and advised to pick up someone. This man approached the cab and stated, "Are you waiting for whatever his name was?" I replied, "Yes." He took a seat in the cab and told me to take him to the Baltimore Gas and Electric building downtown. We started talking and he stated, "Would you believe that I have a gas and electric bill for $500.00?" I stated, "Man you gotta be kidding! What are you paying, the bill for the last six months?" He said, "No! This is a two-month bill."

Then the man started talking about conflicts between him and his landlord concerning the bill. He revealed that the landlord was a bastard and that he thinks the landlord is heating his office from his utilities. Then he stated that it was difficult for him to prove. I asked, "Did you attempt to find out if the landlord had a separate meter for his office?" He said that he could not find one. I advised him to contact BG&E and have them look for the meter, or he could have the bill challenged regarding its validity. He stated that BG&E didn't give a fuck - that all they wanted was their money. I told him, "That is partially true, but if you challenge the bill, they will have to justify your consumption."

When we arrived downtown, he asked me to wait. When he returned to the cab, he stated that he wanted to return to Eutaw Place. While riding, we started talking about how tough it was to make some big money in this white world. When I arrived on Eutaw Place, I stopped on Lafayette Avenue and we continued our conversation about money. He asked if I would like to come in for a beer. My first reaction was no, but after talking for a while, I gave him an affirmative answer. After parking the taxi, we walked to the alley of a different block. I stated that I thought that you lived in such-and-such a block. He stated that he didn't want taxi drivers to know exactly where he lived. So whenever he ordered a taxi, he always had it dispatched to a location in close proximity to his apartment. **No doubt about it, this man was either hiding something or he was paranoid.**

We entered his apartment from the rear. I had never been to New Orleans, but the arched wrought iron gate, back yard, and patio looked like something that one would find down there. The man's crib was actually beautiful. It had all types of antiques and oriental rugs, spiral stairwell, high gloss hardwood floors, and historical paintings. This man was black, but I could definitely see that he was reared in a white setting. I was extremely impressed and felt like asking him who the fuck he was? I have been around and consider myself a worldly person, but I have *never seen a single person's apartment with such a high scale of elegance and grandeur. The first floor and basement were as large as a six-room house. The first floor rear had a sliding glass door separating the house from the patio. This dude stated that he was a law student, appeared to be about twenty six years old, and he impressed me as being extremely rich. This man's wine collection was "terrible," I mean it was "baaad." He had wines on his shelf I had never heard of. His literary collections were equally impressive. He was without a doubt more well read than most of the niggers in Baltimore combined.*

He stated that he had moved to Baltimore recently from somewhere out west. He talked to me about chartered flights to Central and South America. Then I asked myself if this man was into dope, but he didn't offer me any drugs. He also talked about his housekeeper. He finally offered me a drink, and we started talking about women and the troubles they can cause. This guy really had me baffled; I could not figure him out. He didn't impress me as a fag, but something was very peculiar. I think his real problem was that he was lonely and in need of genuine friendship. **In the taxi business, you often meet people who just want someone to talk to.** *However, while we were talking, he showed me some pictures from South America. We later went into the yard, where he started his cast iron layered grill with hickory wood chips. He cooked some ribs and asked if I would stay for dinner. I am always looking for a free meal, so my reply was sure. At this point, his lady came in and said hello to both of us. She went inside, changed her clothes and started watching television. When the ribs were ready, he set up a round table on the patio with a floor length tablecloth, lit a candle and placed it on the center of the table. He set the table for two. My guess was that the lady wasn't invited. He fixed her a plate and took it inside. While inside I heard him tell her to hold his calls until after dinner. When he returned, I asked if the lady was going to join us for dinner. He said that she would eat inside. I* *said to myself that I really heard that! Then the man told me that she was all right but that they really were not on the same wave length. He stated that the reason she stayed with him was because he like to keep a chick around at all times. After dinner, I excused myself and told him that I had to return to work. This man definitely had values and class. I love living in elegance and being impressed, but his scale of living appeared to be far greater than mine. I believe to some degree that we were on the same wave length, although, with all the man appeared to have going for himself, he seemed lonely or troubled about something.*

Some people just do not give a shit! They may have just experienced something traumatic in life and the cabbie is the first to be encountered after the incident. Some people are so bottled up with anxieties that if they do not talk to someone, they will explode.

This black dude hailed me at the intersection of Pennsylvania and Laurens. He told me to take him to North and Linden Avenues. He revealed that he was just released from Lewisburg Prison last week. I asked him, wasn't that a Federal Prison and what type of crime had he committed? He would not reveal what he went to the joint for. He started talking about all the politicians and heavy drug people that he had met while institutionalized. He stated that his parole officer had set him up with a job but told me that he wasn't fucking with no job. He stated that he knew some big people in some big places and that they were definitely going to look out for him. He started talking about all the people who were heavy into drugs in and out of the joint. I mean this dude was dropping some names. I asked him was he institutionalized for drugs. His reply was "yes". He revealed that he was going right back into the drug distribution world and make some big cake!

In this city, cab driving is not considered a profession. People regard cabbies as dropouts in life or doing this type of

work for the time being until better things in life start happening. They believe that many cabbies want to rip you off, get what they can and will tolerate anything as long as those "bucks" keep adding up. They figure that whatever they say, even if of a criminal nature, it will not go any further, which is basically true. A cabbie is interested in making money and not tying up his time reporting people's personal problems to the proper authorities.

After driving a cab for three years nothing about people's actions or behavior would surprise me. Taxi driving has contributed to some wild experiences in my life. Absolutely nothing would surprise me about man's secrets, habits, or behaviors. As a human being, a cabbie can sometimes get caught up in the flow of life emanating from his experiences. In so doing, he exhibits some of the same human traits. Cases in point are three typical days in my life as a cabbie.

DAY I

I was cruising in the 400 block of East Baltimore Street, otherwise known as the BLOCK or the red light district of the city, when hailed by this white man about 70 years old. Once this man was seated in the taxi, I later found out that he was intoxicated. He gave me a $20 bill and requested me to find him a reasonable hotel. I placed the $20 under the clip on the clipboard, not knowing if this entire $20 was going to be mine or not. The drunk may later start some shit about his money, so I kept it right in his eye sight. While driving, I asked him where he was from and he stated "Ignorance". My reply was, "What?"
He then stated his mother and father. Then he stated,"Did I ask you where you were from?"
I told him that I was just trying to make conversation, since he had instructed me to find him a cheap hotel, and that I figured him to be from out-of town. I apologized and asked him to please excuse me for being friendly. He then started talking, saying, that is the trouble with people today, they are always worried about the other person and not themselves.
This guy really opened up after his initial bullshit. He talked about how man will never be able to conquer the elements of nature, referring to rain, wind, snow, water,

and the disasters caused by them. He went on to talk about a family, revealing if a person has five children, that there is always one child that the parent will cater to - revealing that you may love all five children equally but that you will favor one in the lot. I found this guy to be quite interesting.

Our conversation revealed him to be a Baltimorean, but he wanted a hotel to clean himself up and to watch the football game. The man appeared to want his peace and quiet for a while. I took him to the New Motel located on East Monument Street. Once at the motel, he asked me to go inside with him and help him to register. He stated, "You have the money for the motel registration don't you," referring to the $20 that he had given me when he first entered the taxi. After getting him registered, his cab bill was $4.50, so I told him $5.50. He scraped up five singles and the silver. I then asked, "What about another buck for my troubles?"

He stated "Hell man, I don't have any money, I just have enough to get another bottle." After all that bullshit, you know I barely got the taxi fare from the man.

* * *

This fare alighted at the New Motel on East Monument Street. While attempting to leave the grounds, this lady hollered to me from the second floor landing. When she entered the taxi, I could see that she was a lady of the street. She told me to take her to North and Charles Street. This lady had some terribly large boobs for her size. She was quiet for a while. I noticed her looking at my Public Service Badge and she asked, "How do you pronounce your name?" My reply was, " Thad-de-us."

She laughed and said, "How odd." I asked, what was hers, and she stated, "Honey." I told her, "I have been around, now what is your real name?" She replied, "Bar-bara". I asked her how long had she been in the business and she said, seven years. Then I asked her, "What bizarre behaviors have you encountered with your tricks?" She stated that one man wanted her to tie his balls up and pull the ends of the cord until he hollered. Then she stated that this man wanted her to beat him with a stick until he bled. Another man told her to pee in a glass, then she watched him drink it. She concluded by stating just the other day this black dude wanted her to shit in his mouth. I stated **"Oh come on, I don't believe no shit like that"**. *I told the prostitute that I had read about* **shit like that** *but I had never known of anyone who had experienced those types of acts. From once being a vice cop and now a cabbie, I knew that some people are big freaks. After listening to this chick, I knew these freaky acts that some desire can only be performed on or by prostitutes.*

* * *

Bidded on a call in the 1100 block of Calvert Street. This white couple in their twenties entered the cab and requested me to take them downtown. At times, I become so relaxed that I really don't look at my fares once they are seated. At the intersection of Preston and Charles Streets, I turned to say something to the fare regarding his destination and to my surprise I was confronted by this five foot long boa constrictor snake which was wrapped around the top of the man's body. The snake's tongue was flicking back and forth in its mouth. I really didn't know what to say, nor did I know what to do. But I was cool. I didn't lose control of the taxi. My major concern at that time was to get these people to where they wanted to go as fast as possible and to get that thing the fuck out of my cab.

I became hungry, so I decided to stop at Lexington Market for lunch. I parked the taxi illegally in front of the market on Eutaw Street and went inside. When I returned to the taxi, I found this black woman about fifty years old standing around the vehicle. She asked me to transport her to North Avenue and Druid Hill. This lady was real scroungy looking. She had her wig on backwards, a half pint of gin in her hand; her clothes were smelly and dirty, and she had on a pair of pants under her dress which were falling down. When I approached the taxi I noticed a liquid coming from the rear of the taxi on the driver's side. I immediately looked under the taxi to see if it was leaking fuel or something. At the rear of the taxi, I observed a large puddle which was urine. I asked the lady after she was seated in the vehicle if she had peed behind the car. Her reply was, "Mister I didn't mean any harm, but I had to go real bad."

I was furious. I had just purchased my lunch, her odor was nauseating, and now she told me that she had urinated in public while using my taxi as her shield. I asked her politely to please get out of my cab. Then I felt a bit embarrassed for this lady, but I stuck to my guns. I did not want her in my taxi. How in the world could this lady of fifty years of age or more, pull her clothes down in broad day light, in front of the Lexington Market and pee, especially with people walking up and down Eutaw Street going about their daily business.

* * *

I picked up this lady at Holiday Inn downtown. She told me that she wanted to go to the Rets Electronics School on South Eutaw Street. En route, the lady stated that she normally walks but on this day it was just too hot to lug her heavy baggage. I asked her if she was a salesperson, and she stated that she took book orders for a mid-western college affiliated with Rets. At the school the lady paid the two dollar fare. "Am I supposed to tip you?" she asked. "It's customary," I replied with a smile.

"How much?" "Fifteen percent of the bill or anything in excess," was my reply. She gave me fifty cents and told me she felt so embarrassed.

* * *

I was stopped at the traffic light at the intersection of Cold Spring Lane and York Road. While stopped, I noticed this lady with three children in need of a cab. As she entered the vehicle, I could see that she had been crying. Once seated, she instructed me to transport her to the 2700 block of Harford Road. The lady said, "Excuse me mister for crying but my brother just called from my mother's house revealing that our sister who was an epileptic had just drowned in the bath tub."

The lady then said, "Oh my God! My mother is in church and I don't know how she is going to take it!" She then said, "Let me get myself together, what should I do?" I told her to call for an ambulance and contact the police immediately. At the mother's house, the lady gave me a $20 bill and told me to go and get her sister who lived out Sinclair Lane. It was revealed that the sister had no phone. I was instructed to give her the change when I returned.

En route to the Sinclair Lane address, I could not figure out for the life of me what to say to this lady concerning her sister's death. Quite frankly, it had not been confirmed that the woman was dead and it was not my place to tell her anyway. It didn't come to me what to say until I arrived at the sister's house. After rapping on the door, the sister answered and I told her that her oldest sister instructed me to tell her to get her children and come to their mother's immediately concerning an emergency. She asked, "What type of emergency?" My reply was, "Miss, I don't know, I am just a cab driver." She then said okay and that I would have to wait until she got herself together. About five minutes later, the woman entered the cab with her children.

While returning to the Harford Road address, our conversation was general. My inquisitive mind contributed to the lady talking about her family, revealing that she had four sisters, and that one was an epileptic. When I turned on to Harford Road, two cop cars were parked in front of the mother's house. The lady said "I don't know what's happening, but I don't like this shit".

While attempting to park, the sister that gave me the $20 bill ran up to the taxi and told the lady that their sister so-and-so was upstairs dead, floating around in the bathtub. The lady screamed, jumped out the cab and asked why wasn't someone watching her while she was bathing. The *lady who originally had flagged the cab collected her change from the twenty and they went into the house together. I was saddened concerning the experience. Maybe the woman's life could have been saved if someone would have pulled her out the bathtub immediately and had given her CPR while summoning an ambulance.*

Man, I tell you as a cabbie, some of these people have no regard for you at all!

Had this fare in the cab traveling west on North Avenue, slowing for the red light at Aisquith, when this hopper approached the fare's side of the cab and said, "Look-a-here Man, let me ride as far as Mt. Royal Terrace and I will split the fare." I didn't believe what I was hearing. How could someone approach a perfect stranger in a cab, who had been riding for several blocks and ask him to share his meter? Plus the hopper didn't give a shit about me as the operator of the cab. I guess he didn't or doesn't realize that I am an independent businessman and when I'm in the driver's seat, what I say goes! When the traffic light changed, I tried to run over the hopper's toes.

* * *

Picked these four people up at Harford Road and Federal Street. They told me that they wanted to go to the New Theatre. I told them that if they're going to see **"Fist of Fury",** *that the lines were long as shit. That was a big mistake on my part; I will never do anything like that again in my life. All I am doing is cutting my own throat. I have to learn to keep my mouth shut and transport people wherever. I figure this type of behavior to be deceitful but what are you supposed to do when you're hustling for a living. In actuality, I could have lost $5.00. After saying what I did to these people I had to play it down to some degree.*

* * *

This couple called to me from a porch in the 2800 block of the Alameda. The couple was about 55 years old. They told me to take them to the Marylander Hotel on Pulaski Highway. While driving, I heard this old fart of a lady state to the man, when I get you to the hotel (I mean motel), that she was going to treat him the way the Lord meant for a woman to treat a man. I felt like turning around and asking, "How is that?" Then the lady stated that she was hungry and that she wanted some chicken from Gino's on Pulaski Highway.

While the lady was in Gino's the man told me that she was a good old girl and that he had been fucking her for years. He then told me that she was his wife's best friend. I said, "What?" I asked him did he feel uncomfortable when they are together. He told me, "Hell no!" I asked did his wife know about her and he said, "No." I told him that I didn't think that I would be able to handle that! After the couple had departed, I wondered how secrets like that could go unnoticed by a spouse.

* * *

*Picked up a merchant who was an African in the Fells Point section of the city. He told me that he wanted to go to his ship somewhere around the Hanover Street Bridge but before transporting him there, he wanted to know where he could purchase some **reggae music**. I told him about this place called Record and Tape Collectors located in the northern section of the city. He instructed me to take him there.*

*While en route, I asked this guy what part of Africa was he from. He stated that his home was the Ivory Coast. This guy's conversation was interesting. He spoke glowingly about Africa and his English was excellent. He informed me that a package of cigarettes in the Ivory Coast cost more than marijuana. I asked him how was African grass. He replied **"Excellente."** He then asked me did I know where he could purchase an ounce for a good price. I advised him that I knew a lady that sold some good weed. He asked could I take him pass her place after leaving the record shop. My reply was, "Sure." For the expression "watch out" the African* would say "mind you." I thought that was cute. After the African had purchased his music, I took him pass the lady's so that he could get his dope. To my surprise, the dope lady wasn't in. I apologized and told the African that this was unusual that the lady wasn't home. He stated that it was all right, just take him back to his boat. After we had found the ship, the African's final fare was twenty nine dollars.

* * *

I stopped at the traffic light at the intersection of North and Pennsylvania Avenues. These three black girls, who were not more than fifteen years old hailed the cab. One was carrying a young child on her hip. The child was sucking on a baby bottle hanging from her mouth. Another girl appeared to be in about her ninth month of pregnancy. They requested me to take them to Lanvale and Mount Streets. En route I was concentrating on my driving and really wasn't paying much attention to their conversation. But I heard one girl say that she could not wait until Christmas because someone was giving her a gold tooth. I looked in the mirror and noticed that the little chick had silver chewing gum paper wrapped around her front right tooth to impress her peers. However, I realize that many black children damage their perfectly good front teeth as a "fad." Many inner city blacks both old and young, sport gold teeth. This is a tradition of life for some in the ghetto!

* * *

Picked up this family at North Avenue and Pulaski Street. They stated that they wanted to go to Mondawmin Mall. When the man got into the taxi, he had in his possession what appeared to be a portable radio. As I proceeded to drive, I heard the man ask his son if he wanted to watch the **"Dukes of Hazzards"**. I thought that he was asking the child if he wanted to watch the show when they got home. All of a sudden I heard the "Dukes" on television. When I was able to, I turned around and noticed this *screen protruding from the black portable case and the whole family diligently watching television. At the Mondawmin Mall, the man retracted the screen into the case and paid the fare.*

* * *

I picked up this job at Fremont Avenue and Saratoga Street. After the man entered the taxi, he revealed that he wanted to be transported to Barrington Road and Garrison Boulevard.
En route he started talking about his ex-girlfriend's father who had just died. He further stated that he was not notified about the death. He revealed that he received the notification after the burial. While driving up Liberty Heights Avenue, the passenger noticed a man walking a dog. You might not believe this, but for the next fifteen minutes, this passenger talked to me about dog shit. He told about this neighbor of his, a policeman, who walks his dogs daily and that the dogs always shit on his front lawn.
The man really had me laughing, talking about steam coming from the dogs' shit and about the big and little dogs' turds. He told me that he had confronted the policeman on several occasions about his dogs shitting on his lawn. He said he was told by another policeman in the area to call the police and report the incident. I advised him that if he didn't get any results from the police department, to report the matter to the Baltimore City Health Department. He told me that he revealed to the policeman that if it happened again that he was going to shoot the dogs. Then he stated that he didn't know why people walked dogs. This got me to thinking, ***"Why do people walk dogs? Are they lonely, or do they just want to get away from their spouse and children for a while?" Maybe dogs to them are what W. C. Fields would call "an extended metaphor for an inferiority complex," or may be this is a period of solitude for those involved.***
This man was really upset over the dog shit problem and

as a prior homeowner I could understand where he was coming from.

* * *

One might be surprised concerning the amount of illiteracy in the city. I was transporting this black woman up to the Park Heights Avenue area. On Auchentoroly Terrace, this woman read the speed limit sign aloud saying, "Speed limit thirty miles per hour, checked by radar." She then asked me, "What does that mean? Do little wires come out the lamp poles and check the speed of the cars?" I then explained to the woman how the police were able to check the speed of cars. After explaining this to the woman, 1 thought to myself, ***"Does this type of ignorance stem from lack of exposure, or what?"*** *This made me realize that some people just live and really don't know what is happening in the world.*

* * *

I was hailed by this black man at the intersection of Popular Grove and Edmondson Avenues. He told me to take him to Clifton and Ellamont Street. After the dude became comfortable, he started talking about how bad he was and that whatever city he lived in, his hands had to be registered. The man was intoxicated, but he appeared to be solidly built. He told me that he held a black belt in karate and that he was tops in his field. The man was built, but he didn't appear to be in shape for anything. He just kept talking about his hands and how powerful he was. At the man's destination, it was a bitch trying to get him out of the cab. He kept talking about his hands. Then the man said that he had no pain in his hands and proved his point by letting three to four matches burn out at a time in the palm of his hand. 1 had never seen anything like that. 1 told him that he belonged in the circus.

* * *

Picked this job up at Edmondson Avenue and Bentalou Street. He stated that he wanted to go to the 6000 block of

Western Run Drive. The guy talked like he was from the bottom of the ghetto but he was okay.
We started talking and he stated that he was going to a pajama party. He went on to state that three buddies were supposed to go with him but they flaked out at the last minute. He stated that he had purchased the pajamas in his bag just for the occasion. I asked him was he actually telling me that he was going to a male-female pajama or slumber party? I also asked him was he for real? I said this type of party had to turn into an orgy. He told me, "I bullshit you not." He requested that I stop at Park Heights and Belvedere so that he could purchase some beer for the party. When he returned to the taxi, he gave me a beer.
Once at the Western Run address, I asked if he would mind if I accompanied him into the party. He stated that he didn't give a fuck. After finding the apartment, there was a red sign on the front door revealing "sex haven of the world, enter at your own risk." I had never seen anything like that on a person's door in my entire life. This nice looking light-skinned chick, dressed in a night gown answered the door telling us to please come in. Once in the apartment, the chick asked us where were our pajamas. The passenger stated that his were in the brown bag, and I revealed to the chick that I am a taxi driver who had chauffeured so-and-so to the party. I told the lady that I was curious about what so-and-so had told me, and I wanted to check the party out. Two other ladies clad in street clothes were putting party stuff around the walls. I asked where were their pajamas and they stated that they were in the back room.
This other lady, who appeared to be the hostess, was cooking all types of food in the kitchen. The hostess told me, "The rules are that you have to have a pair of pajamas to stay." I revealed to her that I didn't wear pajamas, but if she liked, I would go home and attempt to find something appropriate for the occasion. While leaving, the ladies told me to bring back as many men as I

could possibly find, but under no circumstances, don't bring back any women.

After leaving, I said to myself that this was too much to believe. **Then I thought to myself about the places a cab can take a person.** *I rode around the streets for another hour, then I turned the cab in. I returned to my apartment, found some old raggedy-assed pajamas that had to be fastened with a safety pin and a Hollywood tee shirt that I had purchased from my trip to California, plus a long sleeve underwear shirt. I got my little bit of weed that I had around the house and left for the party.*

When I arrived in the vicinity of the party, I could barely find a place to park. Before entering the apartment, I looked through the front window and noticed some twenty-five or more women clad in pajamas and about three men. I thought twice before knocking on the door, but I went ahead and knocked anyway. Once inside, this light skinned chick stated, "So you have returned."

I was immediately shown to the bathroom. Once there, I just sat on the toilet with my clothes on, attempting to get my nerves together to put those raggedy-assed pajamas on and walk out there in this strange place among those strange-ass people. I started to smoke a joint to get my nerves together, but someone rapped on the bathroom door. I put my shit on and combed my hair. I placed my street clothes in my travel bag, walked out of the bathroom, and placed my bag in the backroom. There were some thirty bags in that room. I was nervous among these strangers and actually inched up the wall to the room where the people were. Once there, the hostess offered me a glass of wine and gave me a rolled joint. She stated, "The food is in the kitchen when you are ready for it."

The living room contained mostly women. They were all in a circle. One lady was in the middle telling nasty jokes. All of the ladies in the circle had the floor at one time or another. They all talked about screwing. I asked the lady next to me what this was all about, and she stated nothing but a slumber party. I then asked her whether she knew any of these people, and her reply was, "A few, but *basically, no."* Gradually men were coming into the party. One guy stated, "Good evening, I don't know anybody, but my name is whatever." I felt like saying, "Welcome to the club."

I inquired of other people, but no one seemed to know anyone else. I asked the same lady that I had spoken to earlier what happened at these parties. She said, "You dance, talk, play games, eat, fall asleep, or whatever." I didn't think this lady was telling me what I wanted to hear. I was getting hungry, so I got something to eat. The food was delicious. I smoked some more weed and thought to myself that I had never been to anything like this in my life.

Some of the ladies had some beautiful bodies and were wearing the prettiest pajamas. For some reason the atmosphere to me wasn't right. The people seemed to be pushing their backs up against the walls. The crowd did not appear as alive as they should have been. Everybody appeared to be sitting around waiting for something to happen or for someone to make a move. This lady who appeared to be the oldest, clad in these bunny rabbit pajamas, kept giving me the eye. A record came on, and this lady got down on her hands and knees, pucked her ass up in the air and started grinding with the beat of the music. At this point, stag movies came on via some type of television hookup. I knew that this was a dream coming true, but I was becoming paranoid. **I believe that police shit was coming out in me after assessing the situation.** I was in these strange people's house with my pants in another room, the apartment had no back door, plus I appeared to be in a room with a bunch of horny women that outnumbered men eight to one. Thinking to myself what would I do if these bitches got crazy and pinned me down on the floor. I didn't know any of these people and my decision was to get the hell out of there. **I now know how a man feels when he is separated from his pants.**

I asked this chick next to me what was next and she replied that she really didn't know. I said to myself that I am not going to screw anybody in an environment like *this, and if I don't, no telling what these people might do to me. This chick who was clad in the bunny rabbit pajamas had the "hots" for me, but I definitely didn't want that lady. After getting myself together, I went to the backroom, put my clothes on and got the fuck out of there. This was around three a.m.*

Once I was home, I had to call my best lady friend and reveal to her what I had just experienced! She stated, "You are a worldly person, why didn't you stay for the grand finale?" My reply was, "I don't know, but the only thing that I can say is that the atmosphere just wasn't right."

No matter how tired some people are, come Friday night, they have to party. This is attributed to their frustrating work week. They will alleviate their aggravations by exposing themselves to a socially relaxing and entertaining environment. You can actually hear people say, "Thank God it's Friday," and that they cannot wait to get into the streets.

DAY II

I was cruising in front of the Civic Center when I was hailed by this black man who stated that he wanted to go to Preston and Greenmount. While driving, I sensed this peculiar smell coming from this man, but I couldn't place it. The man stated that he had had a rough day on the job and that he was extremely tired. From the smell coming from this man, I had to ask him where did he work. He stated that he was a medical assistant in the morgue. I shut up for a moment, then I stated, "I guess you can cut a person open while eating your lunch."

He said, "Man you can get use to anything." I stated, "Yea, I guess you can." He illustrated by pointing to positions on his body where one has to be cut to remove the brain and heart. I asked him how could he stand watching people get cut open like that! His reply was that somebody has to do it and the money isn't bad. I asked him what happens to the unclaimed bodies after a period of time. He stated that if the cadaver is in good shape, the medical students will experiment with it, and if it isn't,

then it will be thrown into the acid tank. I had to ask how long does it take for a body to dissolve.
He was serious but he was saying it laughingly, "Puff, now you see it, now don't". He also told me that if one should die from an accidental death, no matter who you are, the body must go to the morgue for an autopsy. Stating that the only way the body escapes the morgue, is if the person is under medical care and the attending physician has to sign the death certificate. He also told me that bodies are housed in large refrigerated rooms. Drunks and most cadavers start to develop mole after a prolonged period of time. The conversation was very interesting, but I stopped being inquisitive because this man was giving me the creeps.

Many people will insist upon telling the cabbie that children are not to be counted as individual people, referring to five in a cab and two of the individuals are small children, not in arms. These people are told that the Public Service ruling is a maximum of four passengers per vehicle. They are then told regarding an accident, the insurance courier will only cover four passengers, and that the operator could possibly lose his job. They will say "come on man, it's only a child." The cabbie has to express how sorry he is, but it is not worth his job. Some people will alight from the vehicle cursing the operator.

I picked up five "hopper" girls at the intersection of Preston and Milton. I informed them that the Public Service Commission only allows four in a cab. They stated, "Come on man." I said, "All right, for a dollar extra." One of the chicks replied, "Solid." Someone revealed that they wanted to go to the high rise in the 1000 block of Argyle Avenue.
En route to the Argyle Avenue destination, one would not have believed the language that was coming from these chicks. It was absolutely filthy. These girls were into heavy drugs, burglaries, stealing, and whatever else is illegal. After completing the job, I informed the chick up front that the fare was three dollars and fifty cents plus a dollar extra. The chick up front just opened the door and

got out of the cab. I turned around and the others followed suit, except one. She gave a dollar. She stated, "Wait a minute Mister, this ain't right, I'll get your money for you."

I got out of the cab with the chick and watched the bitches run toward the high rise. I hollered, "Hey you motherfucking whores, where is my god damn money?"

They said, "Fuck you," from about three hundred feet and disappeared into the high rise building. It was a hot evening and there were about thirty niggers in front of the high rise. So I decided to leave well enough alone. I am no fool, and I certainly was not going to get myself fucked up, or killed over three dollars and fifty cents.

* * *

I bidded on a call in the vicinity of Washington Boulevard and Carey Street. I was dispatched to pick up a man named "something" at High's store located at the intersection of James and Carey Streets. Once the individual was seated in the taxi, he instructed me to drive him to the Madison Street entrance of the City Jail. He stated, "You know the side where the big red door is located." He then commented on how much rain we had had and told me to watch those fat-legged women. I asked him, what did he mean? He told me that those fat-legged women from the Block got him in a heap of trouble a couple of months ago. He revealed that he was from Upper Marlborough and that he came to Baltimore a couple of months ago to have some fun on the Block. He said those bitches got him stinky drunk and soaked him for all of his money. Further revealing that he didn't get any ass, and when he left he attempted to drive his car, later getting arrested for drunken driving. I asked him was he represented by a lawyer. He told me that he had hired this old bastard from South Baltimore who wasn't worth shit. He told me when the Judge sentenced him, that he must have eaten shit for breakfast. In the same breath, the man stated that he wasn't going to let it get the best of him. The man said his sentence was 30 days in the

Baltimore City Jail. The judge allowed the man to keep his job and told him that he would have to come into the City Jail one day a week for the next 30 weeks to serve off his sentence. I have never heard of a jail sentence like that, but I told the man that it could have been worse. The real kicker to this whole story was that the man was half drunk going in for his 24-hour sentence.

* * *

*I was cruising east on North Avenue approaching Moreland Avenue when hailed by two black women about twenty-five years old. They took a seat and instructed me to drive them to Mondawmin Shopping Center. The flag on the meter was thrown indicating $1.00 for the initial fare. As I was preparing to pull from the curb, one chick revealed to her girlfriend that there is "so-and-so" who was operating another cab and they immediately got out. I hollered what about my buck for the fare. They told me that I should have waited until I got in traffic before turning the meter on. They just shut the door and walked away. I hollered out the window in anger calling the two, "...black ass bitches, and that's one of the reasons why cabbies won't pick up you **niggers**."*

* * *

This black dude about 25 years old flagged me in front of Food-A-Rama at the Mondawmin Shopping Center. He told me to take him to Liberty Heights and Garrison Boulevard. He said that it's a bitch having a little bit of money. Revealing that he had hit the number for fifty cents and that everybody wants a little piece of his change. Revealed that he was due and had taken all his money and bought a complete new wardrobe. I looked over at him and he had on everything new, including shoes. I stated, "You didn't waste any time trying out your new shit." He told me that he went into Mondawmin's public bathroom and put his shit on immediately! At the dude's destination, he was told that his fare was $2.00. He said, "Goddamn man what are *you trying to do, rip me off." Then he went down into his sock, paid his fare, and stated, "The rest is for a fifty dollar bag of dope." He said, "Man I bangs," pointing to a vein in his left arm. Now this man expressed true ghetto mentality to the fullest extent.*

* * *

Picked up these two well dressed ladies at the intersection of Madison and Lanvale Streets. They told me to take them to the Ritz Nightclub on Light Street. These ladies were between 20-25 years old, spoke well, and appeared to be of good stock. They talked about their male peers on their jobs. One stated how fine so-and-so was, and added that she wanted to give him some leg, and she started squirming in the seat. She told her girlfriend that the only reason she hadn't given him some is because he and somebody were good friends. Then she stated, "You know how men can bad mouth you, but just looking at him, sends chills through my body." She said that if it was not for that male friendship shit, she would definitely give him some, and once again she started squirming in the seat. I turned around, looked at the lady, and gave her a pleasurable smile. I told them that in all my years, I had never heard ladies reveal their sexual desires about men. I stated that I have always heard men reveal that they wanted to do it to some woman, but I had never heard the opposite gender express their preferences so boldly. I continued by stating that most women will remark that they would have to have some feelings and shit for a man, but I had never heard a woman state that she wanted to give a man some on general principles.

The lady then stated that many women are out there, sitting on bar stools, with a case of the hots, looking for a man ... just like a man is looking for a woman.

My reply was, "Oh really, then why do the majority of them turn men down when they ask them to dance, or if he attempts to strike up a conversation?" The reply was, "I guess those individual men just didn't appeal!" The lady pulled out her compact, looked in the mirror, powdered her nose, and stated, "Believe me doll, women are out there for the same reasons as men." At the Ritz Nightclub, the lady gave me a dollar tip, blew me a kiss, and stated, **"Good-night Thaddeus."**

* * *

I was traveling south on Reisterstown Road approaching Belvedere with a fare in the cab. At that location, I noticed this white woman of the street in need of a cab. I hollered out the window, "Where are you going?" She stated, "Downtown." Once seated in the cab, she gave me a five dollar bill and asked would this cover it.
I said, "Sure Baby." The lady really didn't start talking until the previous fare alighted at North and Druid Hill Avenues. Once they were gone, she stated, "I hope that I don't have to fuck with nothing but old men tonight." I asked, "Why was that?" Noticing the bruises on her body, she revealed that this motherfucker tried to kill her last night, telling me that she had picked up this trick at Baltimore and Guilford. After the deal went down concerning the money, he stated that he wanted a blow job. She told him to take her to a local covered parking garage in the downtown area. As the prostitute was blowing the dude, she stated that he started hitting her in the head repeatedly. She jumped up crying and said, "If you are not satisfied, I'll give you your money back but please don't kill me!" She stated that the man started beating her on the legs with a wooden object. Revealed that the only way that she got away was by screaming and someone came toward the car. I told the chick that even though she was a prostitute, she had rights and that she was seriously assaulted. Then I asked, did she get the tag number and her reply was, "Yes". She told me that she reported the incident to the police. I asked why don't you take a couple of days off. She replied that she couldn't at this time because the rent was due. The Preakness was in town and this type of event draws all types of people. I felt sorry for the poor women. ***I don't know what is worst,***

the life of a prostitute or that of a cabbie. Neither profession knows who or what they are dealing with.

* * *

I was cruising in front of Trailways Bus Terminal when hailed by this black man about 27 years old. When he entered the cab, I could see that he had been drinking, smoking or something. He told me to take him to Garrison and Belle Avenues. After he made his request, he hollered out the taxi window to an individual in front of Turk Bar, "Nigger you are a dead man", pointing his finger at the individual. All the way up town, this man kept saying that a nigger ain't shit and no wonder the white man keeps him in his place. The man was furious about whatever had happened to him in the bar. He told me, "Yeah! I been drinking, but this motherfucker had no right talk'n to me the way he did. Plus the nigger throw'd me out of the bar."

The man swore on his mother's grave that he was going to kill that nigger this night. All the way uptown he was continuously beating on the right front door of the taxi, revealing how upset he was and how he was going to kill "that black ass-nigger." Then all in the same breath he talked about going to jail concerning some stupid bullshit. I told the man that they would put him under the jail because he had time to ride uptown, cool out, and think about what he wanted to do. I was advising him that if he killed the man now he could not plead temporary insanity or a crime of passion and get away with it. I advised him that he would be charged with cold, first-degree, pre-meditated murder.

After listening to this individual all of the way uptown, I knew that if he had a gun at the time of the incident, he would have killed the man immediately. By the time this man was at his destination, he seemed to have cooled down. His tone of voice was beginning to calm. We shook hands, and I wished him the best of luck and told him not to do anything that he would regret.

Hey Cabbie

It was about eleven p.m. and I was satisfied with my earnings. The day proved to be profitable. I started heading towards the garage, driving south on Park Heights Avenue, approaching Park Circle. In front of the American gas station, I observed this fashionable looking lady. I stopped the taxi dead in front of her, and asked her if she needed a hack. She stated that she was trying to get downtown to the Ritz, but she really couldn't afford a taxi. I said, "Look, it's cold out there, why don't you get in and we can talk while heading in a southerly direction." She accepted my invitation. While driving the lady stated, "I'm out for the night. I need to cool out. Do you mind if I smoke a joint." "No I don't."

The chick must have pulled out an ounce of reefer from her pocketbook. She smoked a joint. Then I told the lady that I was really heading for the garage. "If you like," I said, "after I turn in my taxi, I'll hang with you for the evening, and we can chill out together."

She mumbled something about catching a four a.m. bus to New York. Then the lady stated, "Aside from having to catch the bus, I won't mind hanging with you for the evening." We rode down to the taxi garage; I turned my hack in and reported my earnings for the day. Then we got into my little green two-seater and headed-off into the night. We were really getting into the weed, and by the time we got to the Ritz, we were real mellow and ready to party. We stayed at the Ritz for a while, then we headed uptown to the **Five Mile House***. At approximately one o'clock, I suggested that we get a bottle of wine, some snacks, and go to my apartment for the remainder of the night. The lady accepted my invitation, and we headed towards home. I picked up a fairly good bottle of wine, a couple pieces of chicken from* **Leon's Pig Pen** *and we went to my apartment. Once there, I broke out some wine glasses, poured two tall glasses, sipped, ate chicken, and got into each other. After the wine, chicken and weed, we were pretty high. Me, I was as horny as a human being could possibly get. The lady turned me on immensely. She was beautiful, sexy and she had a lot of class. I* started kissing the lady. She responded. In a matter of seconds, I was virtually all over her. She was responding, pushing me, pushing me, leading me, controlling me. We were near the couch, standing, embracing, kissing, licking, going ape shit, and hog wild after each other. I eased her down on the sofa, being gentle, trying to be romantic, head reeling, spinning, lost in a world of desire ... thinking of Valentino. I placed my hands on her legs, feeling the soft smooth flesh beneath her silken panty hose. She moaned with desire. My hands moved higher, higher until I reached the vee. We were kissing. She moaned and sighed. The message to me was clear. I fondled her breast through her blouse with one hand, while the other hand continued on its wayward journey toward Venus. I was lost. **All the time I was thinking, "This is it. This is it."** I fondled her panty hose clad stomach; she moaned into my mouth and sucked hard on my tongue. I hooked my thumb into the elastic of the garments and was prepared to make that final yank when my new found friend and lover abruptly stopped, pushed me away and jumped to her feet stating, "I have to go."

"You have to what," I screamed.

"I have to be in New York by nine a.m."

"New York! What in the world are you going to New York for?" I asked. **(I've never been able to understand the control of women. Any man who can persuade a woman, any woman, to do anything against her will has a very special talent.)**

Anyway, the lady stated that she had purchased some type of skinned jacket from a furrier in New York which had to be altered. The jacket was ready, and she was going to the Big Apple to pick it up. I felt like asking her, no telling her, to, **"Tell the motherfuckers to mail the son-of-a-bitch,"** but I didn't.

"Will you please take me to the bus terminal," she asked.

To tell you the truth, I really didn't want to. I didn't feel like it, and besides, I felt betrayed, depleted. I really couldn't believe this shit. I was angry, annoyed, embarrassed, humiliated, drained and no longer horny.

Hey Cabbie

But I liked the lady, so I put my shit on and off we went to the bus terminal. We arrived there about five o'clock in the morning. I wanted to just drop her off and keep on trucking, like I should have done, but I couldn't. I liked the lady and wanted to be in her company as long as I possibly could. I parked the car and went into the depot with her. I wanted to be with her, but there was also a degree of skepticism about her story. I really didn't believe that she was going to New York. Once in the station, to my chagrin, the lady actually bought a round trip ticket to New York. I'd never before done anything on such a spur of the moment in my life. But I liked the lady. I wanted to be with her. So I asked, "Would you mind if I go to New York with you."

"I would love to have you come with me."

I didn't have much cash, so I gave the ticket agent my Master Card and asked for a roundtrip ticket to New York. After squaring away the ticket shit, I went outside and parked my car in the garage directly across the street from the bus station.

I thought that this might be fun, because I hadn't been on a bus in over twenty years. I was wrong. It was one hellifing experience. It was horrible. It was like being in the twilight zone ... it was a total nightmare. This bus had to have contained some of the lowest-class people I have ever seen. They were loud, crude, rude and downright common. The seats were very uncomfortable. Fumes from the bus seeped into the coach, and the bathroom door kept flapping open and shut all the way to New York. The lady went to sleep, but man, I couldn't sleep a wink on that thing. Once we reached New York, the subway and busses were on strike, and all the taxis were hired. So we walked about fifteen blocks to this fur store. I got to thinking that I must really be a sucker for a piece of ass. Here it was Good Friday, and I could have made some good money back home in Baltimore. Instead, here I am up here in New York, walking around with some strange bitch that I'll probably never see again in life once we return to Baltimore. I wanted to ask a stranger to kick me in the ass. Suddenly the lady didn't seem beautiful to me. After she got her coat, we stopped off somewhere and had breakfast. At the restaurant, I called a friend of mine in New Jersey. He stated that there was no sense in stopping off because he had to work. I told him that I would talk to him later, and I also stated that I'd wasted enough money on this date. After the lady had taken care of her business and I had made my futile call to my friend, we headed back to the Port Authority Bus terminal to board our bus back to Baltimore. The bus was so crowded that we couldn't even sit together. At this point, it really didn't matter. The ride back was equal to the ride to New York. It appeared that we were riding on the same bus with the same passengers. **We all went to New York for the same purpose.** *Once we were in Baltimore, we went to the Lexington Market got something to eat, and then I took the lady home! Aside from not getting any ass, I don't even remember the bitch saying thank you for accompanying me to the Big Apple.* **On the positive side, the opportunity to do something that was not planned was really worth a million dollars. However, this was undoubtedly the longest cab ride that I've ever taken!**

DAY III

A lady who was on welfare revealed that when people are cheap, they are only cheating themselves out of life. She talked about living for today and that no one knows what is in store for tomorrow. She revealed that if you do not owe it to yourself, then who owes it to you. She stated that she had no savings, and if she was able to save, it would be at a minimum. The lady made sense to a degree. Money is made for the enjoyment of life and not to be stacked away for a rainy day. **That rainy day may never come.**

I picked up this weird black dude at Reisterstown Road and Hayward Avenue. He was dressed in all black, including black hat and eyeglasses. He told me to take him somewhere off of Hayward Avenue to pick up his wife and child. The dude went into the house after we arrived at the address, picked up his wife and child and returned to the taxi. He opened the rear left door for his wife and child, waited until they were just barely in the cab, then he slammed the shit out of the door. He then walked around the rear of the taxi and took a seat up front. I could clearly see that he was boiling about something. I glanced in the rear to get a glimpse of his wife. What a shock! She looked in sharp contrast to the man. She had all of the appearance of the town's whore, while he appeared to be some kind of religious freak - a cross between Daddy Grace and Elmer Gantry. It was almost midnight. He told me that he had a personal check which he had to cash at a service station.

"At which service station," I asked. "I've never heard of anyone cashing a personal check at a service station."

"Just take me to the station please!" was his reply. I drove him to the station as directed, and when we got there, he hopped out of the taxi with all of the aplomb and fanfare due royalty. He went into the office of the service station to transact his business. His wife said to me, "That is one fucked up man."

I didn't reply or give any hint that I was in the least bit interested in what she had to say. She continued, "For the past year he has been dressing up in that black shit. Every suit he owns is black. He even wears black drawers."

To my amazement, he cashed the check at the Crown Station located at Rogers and Park Heights Avenues. When he got back into the taxi he asked the lady, "What the fuck was the motherfucker doing in the house?"

"He only stopped by for a visit." "Visit my ass. You are lying. All the son-of-a-bitch wanted is your damn pussy."

"Man you are sick, she replied."Even if I wanted to fuck someone, it sure as hell wouldn't be him."

Turning to me the man said, "Cabbie, stop me off by Huffman's Bar for a second." At the Bar, the man got out of the cab, went in and returned with a couple of six packs of beer. He popped the lid off of one in the taxi and stated to his wife, "As soon as I get home, I'm going right back out and get myself some pussy."

"Don't be no fool. You just go right ahead and do that, and I'll take this child back to my mother's and then I'll disappear for a couple of days." This type of behavior kept on until I got them to their destination. The weird dude paid me exactly what was on the meter, not a penny more. He got out of the taxi, once again slammed the door with all of his might, walked hurriedly across the street, leaving his wife and child standing on the curb. This was truly the oddest of odd couples.

* * *

I bidded on this call in the vicinity of Forrest Park Avenue and Garrison Boulevard. I was dispatched to the 4000 block of Fairfax Road. This black lady of about thirty years old entered the taxi and stated that she wanted me to take her to the Seven Eleven store located on Gwynns Falls Parkway. She further stated that she wanted me to wait for her while she shopped, then return her to her place of origin. She stayed in the store approximately fifteen minutes. Naturally the meter was running. Once we were back at her place, I told the lady that the meter fare was four dollars and fifty cents, including the twenty five cents for the service charge for the call. Before she paid me, I explained to her that my last fare took all of my silver and that I only had twenty five cents in change. She gave me a five dollar bill and stated that she didn't have any change in her purse. At this point she said that she would go into the house and get fifty cents.

"I'm only a quarter short. Don't you think that would cover my waiting for you for fifteen minutes while you shopped?" She mumbled a reply under her breath. "Well, you kept the meter running, but that's okay, you can keep the quarter," she stated as a final settlement to our dilemma. After the lady got out of the taxi, I thought and realized that it was my fault in not having enough change, but I said to myself, "The nerve of some people and how they impose on others."

Hey Cabbie

I was cruising south on Howard Street in the vicinity of the State Office complex when flagged by this goofy looking white man about thirty years old. The man had been drinking. He took a seat up front and told me to take him to Pratt and Calhoun. This guy not only was goofy, but he was queer from jump street. He started asking me all of these questions about my personal life. Then the man asked me, "Hey pal, would you like to have some white ass?"

"I'm sorry, if you are talking about your white ass, I'll have to pass on that."

"You colored people have such big dicks, and I want you to burst my ass wide open."

"Come on man, cut that disgusting shit out," I re-plied. Furthermore, I continued, "That's only a myth. What makes you think that a black's dick is any larger or smaller than that of a white?" He didn't answer. At one point the goof went to grab for my genitals, but I blocked his attempt.

"Listen," I told the fruit, "you can talk all of the shit you like, but I advise you to keep your hands to yourself."

All of the way to the man's destination, he kept begging me to fuck him in the ass. After he paid his fare, his final plea was, 'Why don't you come on and fuck me?" I just laughed, requested that he close the cab door, and said, "Good night."

* * *

I'd just left Harbor Place and decided to cruise in the vicinity of the Block. At Commerce and Baltimore, this white sloppily dressed man wearing tennis shoes unlaced, no socks and walking with a slight limp, about fifty-five years old approached the cab and asked was I for hire? After my positive reply, he took a seat and told me to drive him to Three Brothers Bar on Frederick Road.

En route the man appeared a little nervous by his actions but he didn't talk very much. As we approached Three Brothers Bar, the man said that he had a check and asked would I mind waiting for him. I noticed the bar had three entrances when entering the parking lot. So I tried to position the cab on the parking lot to observe all exits if the man would try to duck out on me.

As he left the cab, I saw a government check and envelope in his possession. He told me that it was worth $1,000 dollars. I didn't believe him. The store owner wasn't in and the clerks refused to cash the check. We went to three other check cashing places of his choice and they all refused to cash the check. At this point, I asked him how much is the check really worth and did he have proper identification. The check was worth $2,000 dollars and he had a picture ID.

It was Saturday and I told him to cash a check like that, we had to go to check cashing places in the ghetto. The first place that we stopped was on Garrison Boulevard near Liberty Heights Avenue. They refused to cash the check, requiring two pieces of identifications, even though the man had an age of majority card with his name and address. Personally, I believe that they didn't want to get up off that much cash, plus he wasn't a regular. We worked our way down Pennsylvania Avenue until we got to a liquor store located on Laurens Street. The clerk asked him was this his first social security check and that it would cost $40.00 dollars to cash it. After agreeing to the cost, the man told the clerk that he had been waiting five months for this money. He requested to be paid with fourteen $100 bills and the remainder in fifties. The clerk told him to enjoy it and I told the clerk to put his money in a small paper bag.

Then he went on a shopping tour in the check cashing place. He purchased a knife, two radios, alarm clock, beer, food and asked if I wanted anything. I told him that I wanted money but I would like a grapefruit juice. I now felt relieved, knowing that he had some cash! When he got back into the cab, he said he wanted some crabs and to take him to Bo Brooks on Belair Road. He asked me to eat with him because he didn't want to eat alone. Then he said I'm going to give you a $30 tip over the meter fare.

Hey Cabbie

While stopped for the red light at North and Mt. Royal, three inner city black juveniles approached the cab with their window washing equipment. Two attempted to wash the front windshield and the other started washing the rear window. I told them to back off! The fare said loud enough for them to hear, "I like what they're doing and I'll take care of them." He gave them a dollar apiece, at the same time an oriental female approached me and stuck a long stemmed rose in my face and said, "Roses Sir?" I told her not today but my fare hollered across the seat that he would like one. The cost of the rose was $3.00 and the oriental lady said, "Thank you very kindly Sir." When the traffic light changed, I told the fare that these hustlers are at every major inner city intersection and at times get on your nerves tying up traffic begging for money.

On Bo Brooks' parking lot, he decided to pay what he owed. The meter read $37.00 dollars plus a $30.00 dollars tip. He gave me two fifties and told me to give him $30.00 dollars change. At the restaurant he was eating and drinking booze like it was going out of style. I know he considered himself to be living but I said, "Please don't get drunk on me." The guy weighed about 300 pounds and was sloppy as shit. I knew that I couldn't handle this man if he got drunk. I looked over and noticed that he was wearing a watch on each arm. The thought came across that I had a nut on my hands but I wasn't really worried. I asked him why was he wearing two watches and how old was he? He said that he was 52 and that he liked watches. I asked him how did he get social security at 52 years old. He revealed that he played crazy with the authorities to get the money and that it will keep coming until the day he dies. I said, "That's all right!" I asked him to let me lock the knife that he purchased at the liquor store in the trunk until he got to his destination. He said, "Don't worry, I got the money and I need the knife for my protection." He then said that he wouldn't cause me any harm.

Then he asked me where could he buy a color television? I suggested Luskins on Cromwell Bridge Road. He said, "Man they sell cheap stuff!" I said, "Bullshit, they carry all brand named appliances." So off we went to Interstate #695. En route to the appliance store, the dude was complaining how cheap Luskins was and purchased the cheapest set in the place! He gave the clerk a fit and requested him to test the set before we left the store. He paid for the television with cash, then faced all his bills properly before putting the money back into the bag.

Now he said that he wanted to see what BWI Airport looks like. All I was thinking about was getting another one of those $50 dollar bills. I drove clear around the Beltway from Loch Raven Boulevard to Baltimore Washington Parkway. I said to myself fuck it, he didn't know where he was going, plus he enjoyed riding. Man that digital meter was jumping. He asked about the airport and what it looked like today. I told him that the only part of the old terminal that existed is the tower. He also revealed that he wanted a motel in the vicinity of the airport. At the airport the man was simply amazed! He hung the top portion of his body out the front window and said, "This motherfucker is beautiful." The man said, "Just let me off here." "What about your television," I said. "Oh yea, take me to the closest motel." We went to Hotel International. I went in and they stated that they had no rooms. I told the man what the hotel clerk revealed and said to him that he should try, believing perhaps that she may have been lying because I'm black. She told him the same thing, gave him some conversation, and told him that the rooms cost $75 dollars a night. "That's outrageous," he said! "You people must be crazy." We left there and continued on down the road to Holiday Inn.

He got a room and we inspected it before getting his belongings from the cab. In the room, he sat on the bed, crossed his arms and watched television like a ten year old child. We then went downstairs, had a drink, and listened to a local band. "Let's go settle up," he said.

As we were leaving, I signaled for the baggage lady to assist me with his belongings. While placing this shit on the baggage cart, she said, "Looks like someone is going to have a party. He had his own color television, crabs, beer, and sandwiches. I observed him peeking at the meter which read $42 dollars. We sat down and talked for awhile. He gave me another $50 dollar bill, asked me was that fair, and thanked me for sticking with him for the past four hours. **I told him that I loved every bit of it and said this type of fare is the dream of every cab driver.** *This man gave me $120 dollars which averages $30 per hour. This is the largest cash fare and tip ever in my career as a taxi operator!*

* * *

I observed this lady with her bus driver boyfriend in front of the MTA building located on Washington Boulevard. She noticed me cruising, hailed, and kissed her friend goodbye. She told me that she wanted to go to a nursing home located in the 9200 block of Liberty Road. She gave me one route, and I told her of another one that would be more of a savings to her. En route I started teasing her about her friend and how she had to run off to work. She told me that he operated on the twenty eight bus line, and that she met him one evening coming home from work.
"You have beautiful hair," she interrupted. "Are you married or single?" "A little of both," I replied.
"If I had taken the bus, I would be late, but since I am taking a taxi, I'll get to work very early. Would you like to share a quart of beer with me?" she asked.
"I wouldn't mind at all," was my reply. We stopped near the nursing home, purchased a quart of beer, and searched for and found a secluded spot in which to consume our brew. We drank the beer, smoked cigarettes (Kools) and talked about life. We later started kissing, feeling and rubbing on one another. I attempted to pull her pants down, but she stopped me, stating, "I have to go to work." **The control of women!** *We got ourselves together, and I transported her to her place of*

employment. She paid the ten dollar meter fare and gave me her phone number which is ... **no I'd better not.**

* * *

I picked up this hopper (hoodlum) at Park Heights and Violet Avenues. He was carrying this monstrous radio. After the hopper was seated, he stated that I should chauffeur him to the high rise project located in the 100 block of North Aisquith Street. He went on to state that he didn't have any money on him, and that he would have to go into the high rise to get my "cake." I said, "Hey man, I know that you are going to leave your radio while you go into that place to get my money." I revealed to him that he could go into that place and that I would probably never see him again.

"No problem," *he stated.* "By the way, what is your cab number?" *I gave him the number. While at Park Circle, the hopper changed his mind and told me to take him to Clifton and Pennsylvania Avenues. At that location, he left his radio in the cab, walked towards the poolroom and rapped on the door. Someone answered the door after about three minutes. Meanwhile I'm thinking of how people, especially black people, love to take advantage of your time. So when I do this type of shit, I always leave the meter running. When he got out of the taxi, the meter read two dollars and ten cents. When he returned the meter had advance to two dollars and eighty cents.* "How much is the fare?" *he asked.* "Two dollars and eighty cents," *I replied.*

"Motherfucker, you mean you left the goddamn meter on?" "Yeah! And who do you think you are talking to, you black bastard!" *I told him,* "You are on my time, and it costs ten cents a minute while I'm sitting here."

He stated, "Here man. This is two dollars and twenty cents. I have to owe you the rest." "Owe shit motherfucker," *I said,* "You'd better get the rest of my money!" *He backed away from the taxi, and for a brief moment I didn't really know what to expect. Then I realized that he was going over to ask some old Wine-o for the rest of the money. I started to get out of the taxi, but then I saw the old Wine-o fumbling in his pockets to give him the money. The Wine-o, surprisingly enough, came up with the money. The hopper approached the opened front right door, stood back and threw the silver coins into the taxi. I don't recall specifically how this guy got his radio out of the cab. Regarding what had happened, I just laughed, closed the door, and went on my way.*

* * *

This guy flagged me down in the 700 block of Fulton Avenue. He requested that I take him to the Convention Center. After he got comfortable, he asked, "Do you mind if I smoke a joint?" I recall transporting this guy before, and at that time he had asked me the same shit. I told him, "Sure you may, but it will cost you an extra dollar to smoke that shit in here."

Furthermore, I stated, "I'm sick and tired of niggers getting into my cab, smoking that shit and not giving me a tip. If you want to smoke, then it's going to cost you a dollar." "Hey man," the guy stated, "that's cool. I understand where you coming from. I used to push these things myself one time. The dollar's cool."

The last time this guy smoked a joint in my cab, he didn't give me a tip, nor did he offer me a hit off of his joint. This time I took some hits off the joint, plus I took his dollar.

* * *

I was cruising in the Block, Baltimore Street between Holiday and Gay, the infamous block of sex, when I was hailed by this white man of about twenty. He entered the cab, and I noticed that he couldn't speak English very well. He stated, "I wanna a go to a Pennsylvania Avenue."

This made it even more obvious to me that he was a foreigner.

"Where are you from," I asked.

"I'm from Germany. I come in on ship in Harbor. Ship docked in Harbor. I'm sailor on ship."

"Who told you to go to Pennsylvania Avenue," I asked. "Are you looking for a chick?"

I tried to the best of my ability to explain to him that blacks lived in the area and that was not the ideal place for his white-German-ass to go prowling around in search of some pussy. I used all of my diplomacy. Matter of fact, the State Department would have been proud of me. I told him that one of those bastards on the Block was trying to play a joke on him that could probably get him into some serious trouble, may be even killed. I told him that he would be better off going to the Fells Point Dock section. **(As a cabbie, you have to know these things).** *Somehow or another I got him to understand. At times we were communicating, and at times we were not. When we were not communicating we would look at each other and laugh because we simply couldn't understand each other. So we substituted the universal language.*

At Fells Point, he paid the fare and thanked me. After the guy departed into the night in search of a piece of American nooky, I thought to myself how difficult it would have been for me to sleep peacefully that night if I had taken him to Pennsylvania Avenue. I would have had visions of something happening to him ... visions of reading the morning paper and discovering that his head was found on Pennsylvania and Dolphin. It must be a bitch being in a country and not knowing the language. As a cabbie I encounter many non-English speaking individuals often. This stems from Baltimore being a port city. **I'm seriously thinking about going to night school to learn how to speak Spanish. This is America's number two language.**

* * *

I picked up this white male of about 45 years old in the Fells point section. He wanted to be transported to Essex. He started talking about his domestic matters and how the shit was so bad that he had to leave Baltimore. He

stated that his wife was soaking him for one hundred and fifty dollars a week and that she still wasn't satisfied. He revealed that he made good money as a truck driver, but he couldn't stand his wife asking the court to grant her more, more and more money. So he took all of his savings and left Baltimore to see the country. **I thought to myself that this man sounded like a carbon copy of me, so I had better listen to him closely.** *He revealed that in order to work in Georgia and Alabama one had to belong to the Southern Baptist Church. He said that if you made four dollars an hour, that you really worked your balls off. He told me that he ran out of money and was down to his last suit and a raggedy-assed station wagon. He further revealed that he had to sell both of them in order to survive. He told me that he had some good times, but he was never so glad of anything in his life than to return to Baltimore. He said, "There are a lot of places far worse than Baltimore."*
"I've been out there," I told him, "and I know exactly what you are talking about."

* * *

I was driving back into the city via Eastern Avenue when I was hailed by these chicks in front of City Hospital. These two hillbilly chicks, a white and a mixed breed child entered the cab. They told me to take them to Federal Street right off of Milton Avenue. These people were very ethnic by nature. They had the customs, language, and social views of **niggers**. *One chick talked about how she stole the fasteners the dentist used to keep the smock around her and that she was going to use them as marijuana roach clips. Then she stated that as soon as she got home that she was going to get some motherfucking Thunderbird and smoke a joint. She asked the other* **nigger-billy** *if she had any weed. The chick said, "Yeah," and she pulled it out of her bra along with her money. Then the chick stated, "I want some vodka instead of that fucking 'bird', and if John is there at the house, I want him to do it to me."*

These ladies, or whatever, had terrible mouths, and they had no regards whatsoever for the children. Once at their destination, I looked into the house and observed this black dude sleeping on the living room sofa. I felt like saying to the one lady, **"I guess your wish will come true."** *These people lived in the heart of East Baltimore's black ghetto which contributed to me understanding their mannerisms.*

* * *

It was about 10:15 p.m. and I had made my goal. I was driving west on Fayette Street, en route to the garage. In front of the new Post Office, this drunk came from between two parked vehicles and flagged me. Instinctively I stopped. Before I could really inquire where he wanted to go, the dude was seated in the taxi. The man was drunk and revealed that he wanted to go to Lexington and Monroe Streets. After the man told me where he wanted to go, he fell asleep. While driving, I started thinking to myself, **"The only reason I am transporting this man is greed!"**
This type of bullshit can get a cabbie hurt. At the dude's destination, I woke him up, and stated, "Here we are."
He told me to make a left turn on Monroe and stop midway in the block. He then told me in a drunken manner that he had to go into the house for my money. About ten minutes had passed, and then I exited the taxi and rang the doorbell. A chick answered the door and I asked her where the man was who had just gotten out of my taxi. She stated, "He is in here asleep."
I became furious with the lady, "What? Don't tell me the bastard has me out here waiting for him while he's in there asleep." I entered the house and we both approached the dude in the living room. The lady stated, "What are you going to do about this taxi shit?"
"I dunno. I ain't got no money." The woman then said, "I don't know what the fuck to do neither, cause I sho ain't got no money."   "Listen Mister," I said "I don't want to

have to call the cops, but you don't leave me any alternative."

"Fuck it then, call the motherfucking cops," he replied. I got on the taxi radio told the dispatcher to send me the police. She asked, "Is everything all right?" "Yes at this time," I responded. When the cops arrived, I explained my side of the story. The cops then went into the house and asked the dude was he going to pay the fare. The man told the cops that he didn't have any money, and would the cabbie come back tomorrow.

One cop then asked, "Did you tell him that when you took a seat in the taxi?" The other officer pulled me to the side and stated, "I hate this type of shit. If I lock him up, will you show up for court?" "Sure!" I said.

He placed the man under arrest, and off he went in the paddy wagon. I didn't believe the cops were going to lock him up. I thought they were going to tell me to get a warrant from the court commissioner if I wanted my money. I was notified by mail that the trial date would be a month later. On the day of the trial, the Judge released the man, because he had stayed in jail for the entire month for failing to pay three dollars and fifty cents. I guessed that the man wasn't released on his own recognizance because of his character, nor could he make bail. The fact remains that I'm still out of three dollars and fifty cents, plus I lost time and money dealing with the court shit. His jail term did not make up for my losses!

Everyone in the world has problems, and it is so satisfying in life to know that someone else's is always worst then yours. At times this job is just therapy. After riding around the streets for ten to twelve hours, seeing how many of these people live, and after listening to their hardships, no matter how depressed or down you may have been, your problems are miniscule compared to theirs.

Driving a taxi is an experience of a lifetime. Driving a cab really makes one aware of people's habit, customs and cultures. If one is open-minded and has nerve, one can gain firsthand experience of how others exist. A cabbie's awareness stems from transporting and becoming involved with a cross section of the citizenry of Baltimore, or of the city where he serves. **You learn the "whys" of people's actions and how to "rock and roll" with them in a commonly shared cultural society.** Knowing that all humans have to eat, sleep and eliminate, and knowing that they need shelter, clothing, and knowing that their environmental situations, learned values, and acquired dignity constitute their level of success in society is common knowledge. However it is just that people go after the ultimate goals concerning survival in life in so many different ways.

Cabbies transport a very precious commodity, and that is a human being. There is no replacement should serious injury come to those individuals while under your immediate control. It is absolutely imperative that all precautions of motor vehicle safety are adhered to while chauffeuring fares. If not, the repercussions could be devastating.

A professional cabbie is a hustler and a manipulator of people. He will do many things to get that buck, or that extra buck. They possess erratic driving behaviors, but in reality they are superb, excellent and professional operators. Although they make U-turns anywhere, quick right and left turns, jump yellow and red lights in anticipation of the green light, stop on a dime for a hailing fare - looking for the police in the vicinity before making illegal turns at controlled intersection - they defy all rules and regulations concerning traffic laws, but statistics show a low rate of serious accidents concerning cabbies. Their accidents for the most part are nothing more than fender benders.

All cab operators within the past two years have had to constantly veer around "subway construction" in the west and northwest section of the city. Many inner city blacks hate the idea of the project and state that its construction will only benefit the whites. They say it is like busing - you bring people into the city from outlying counties for work and pleasure, then you rush them back blindly to their "safe and sterile" environments. They also complain about how the subway construction has contributed to the deterioration of the surrounding streets where the system is being built. People talk of how fast it was built and express their fears that the ground will cave in once it is underground. The construction of a subway system in Baltimore has many advantages. It has created jobs for many. The commercial areas surrounding the underground stations are going through redevelopments - shopsteading, laying of antique bricks, sidewalk repairs, and other beautification projects - in preparation for the day when people will flock to these areas. Although the subway will consist of eight miles at this time, it will be a plus for the city, and everyone will enjoy it.

From listening to my patrons, the public transit situation appears to be a serious problem. They complain of poor service periods, and they generally state that Sundays and holidays are the worst ever. Many inner-city people who depend on public transportation reveal that the service is bad during peak and off-peak hours. They say the fares are high and the service is terrible and that in the summer time the buses are hot, smelly, and the air conditioners never work. Many regular riders have bus passes, and at times they have to hail cabs because of the inconveniences the transit company has placed on them. It is nothing on any given day to see bus patrons getting off an inoperative bus to board another one. On cold days, buses run in tandem, three or four in a group instead of on schedule. Many times bus drivers wait at the end of a route to play a friendly game of checkers before heading back on the job. Meanwhile the patrons suffer. Many people, old and young, sick and well, will scream, holler and risk having a heart attack running after that bus. Some drivers are nasty; see the people running, then pull off anyway.

I was approaching Park Avenue while driving on North Avenue and noticed this nice looking black lady who appeared to be in need of something (cab or bus) looking quite distressful. As I neared her, she was quite indecisive, but she flagged me anyway. Once seated in the cab, she said that she wanted to go to Loch Raven and Cold Spring. She then lit a cigarette and said, "These bus passes are almost worthless during rush hours and weekends. The buses never adhere to their time schedules and many times they break down, causing additional lost time."

The woman is absolutely right. As a cabbie, I see disabled buses more often than I see disabled cars. You can see them all over the city. I then asked the lady, "How much are the monthly passes?"

"Twenty-eight fifty for zone one. Many times it is just a waste of your money, because when you need them the

most, they are not there. You can't even depend on them to get to work on time."

After the lady paid her fare, I said, "Maybe once the subway system is operative, maybe, just maybe, our transportation system will be more efficient." I thought to myself later, **I hope they don't break down underground as often as the buses break down on the streets of Baltimore.**

* * *

While waiting at the light at Harford Road and North Avenue, I noticed this elderly white lady, she had to be at least eighty five years old, hobbling along trying to catch the number thirteen bus going west on North Avenue. She was yelling, flailing her arms attempting to catch the bus. She got to the bus and banged on the door just as the light changed. The driver looked at the old lady and pulled off. The old woman stood on the corner, clenched her fist and yelled, "Happy New Year you-son-of-a-bitch." I felt so sorry for the old lady, so I gave her a ride down North Avenue as far as I was going.

It is very frustrating for a cabbie to bid on or be dispatched to a call for service and the people have left. This is a waste of time, gas, and possibly money because you are passing up fares on the street. Some people will call more than one company and you can guess the rest of that story. Others change their mind and will not bother to call the company to cancel. These are patron traits that cabbies learn to deal with in the industry.

Driving a cab makes you realize that you are only one person and can only do but so much. A cabbie's salary depends on his hustling abilities and what the economy yields at a particular time. No matter how smart one works, one can only be at one place at one time. Now! How intelligently he uses that time will determine his margin of profit. Situation: If Memorial Stadium is letting out and one can hustle more than one fare going to BWI Airport, it is to his advantage. This action will contribute to time and gas saved, plus additional monies can be made for the same efforts. By the time the cabbie would have returned to the stadium, the crowd would have been long gone. In this industry, one must think in order to make that buck.

Professional cab drivers just float from one company to another when they get terminated. The primary reasons for termination are too many accidents, or not paying money owed to the company. These types of drivers seem to retain the same type of reputation where ever they are employed.

One cannot judge a fare by its cover. Sometimes one can presume where a fare wants to be transported, but that is not always true. They hail you, and you think that they are going one place, but in reality they are going someplace else. The scroungiest dressed person could be one of the most highly intelligent and nicest persons and vice versa. The same applies to tipping habits. There is just no formula to determine who is going to give you that extra money. **Prejudice is a BITCH, and we all possess it!**

I was cruising east on Monument Street, when hailed by this black man dressed in a sanitation uniform. He revealed that he wanted to go somewhere on Caroline Street. While transporting he talked of his rough night playing cards, and he said that he had to leave the game in order to report to work by 3:00 a.m. He talked of how tired he was. The final meter fare was two dollars. The patron gave me five dollars and told me to keep the change. This type of action reveals that you cannot judge a book by its cover. I had no idea that this individual was going to give me a three dollar tip.

In this industry it does not take long to realize that money is the root of all evils. Within the industry one realizes that monetary tokens of appreciation breed expedient supportive services and favors to and from everybody. Many do not want to admit it, but that is just the way it is in this society as a whole. It will never change.

Pertaining to the owner/lease of cabs, the taxi meter serves as a guide concerning fares and will solve many fare dispute problems. Example: Fare disputes during heavy traffic and people who refuse to pay because they think the fare is excessive. One should always throw the taxi meter flag. Many people cry about the fare no matter what it is.

Presently inflation is really hurting the industry. Baltimore's unemployment is very high per capita of people. The business is rough; cabbie's earnings are based on what the economy bears. There just isn't much money in circulation today!

As stated earlier, cabbies learn that money is spent in patterns within a month. The first week of every month is always good. This is when government welfare and retirement checks are placed in circulation. These people have to be transported to banks, food markets, and some to their permanent addresses regarding their checks. During the middle of the month money is wisely spent. The weekends will contribute to people letting go of their money. People will spend heavily leading into holidays. Regarding the last week of the month, money is very tight.

During the week some cabbies will rely on organizations that have accounts with the cab companies. When it is slow some money can be found around hospitals, hotels, bus stations, train station, and by concentrating in and around the downtown area. Let no one fool you, this industry does depend on limited income individuals who receive relief and other social services checks.

People think that cab driving is an easy occupation or a means to make a fast buck. All I can say as a cabbie is it is a "bitch" how hard you will have to push yourself for money and "some of the shitty" individuals you have to deal with. A cabbie who works under the owner/lease system works ten to twelve hours, and once he has picked up his manifest and cab, basically there is no turning back or saying "I am sick." Many times you will find yourself sick, tired, or falling asleep at red lights. Sometimes you will have to park the cab and take a fifteen minute nap just to get yourself together. At times you will find yourself exposed to a lot of stress and strain just to make the man's money. It can be rough. A cabbie has to concentrate on his driving and other drivers' habits and keep a constant vigil on the passenger. The patron may want to get engrossed in conversation and at times maybe looking for advice. The cabbie must look out for pedestrians and take the most direct route to the fare's destination. Sometimes you have to role play in order to calm or relax the patron. **People and their problems - we all have them.**

These three white women hailed me from a bus stop located in the unit block of East Baltimore Street. The ladies were slightly high from whiskey. Once seated, they started talking amongst themselves. I heard one of them state that they couldn't understand grown adult sisters being envious and hating each other. One lady started talking to me, and she stated, "You must hear everything as a driver."

Then she went on to reveal that they were sisters, and they loved one another; they were out at a downtown nightspot having a little fun. They were dressed very neatly; the oldest was about thirty-six and the youngest was twenty-eight. One asked, "Do you have sisters and brothers?" "Yes" I replied. "Where do you fit in the lot?" I told her that I was the oldest of five. She wanted to know whether or not we got along. I replied, "All of the boys seem to get along, but the girls appear to be a little distant." "Well as sisters, we get along well and we also love each other very much." "That's beautiful," I replied. "It's nice seeing three adult sisters finding the time to go out on the town and have some fun." **As a black, I don't see much of this among black siblings.** *They gave me a two dollars and fifty cents tip when they got to their destination.*

* * *

Every cab driver occasionally takes a fare for a ride, but on this particular day I kind of over did it. The lady flagged me on East Cold Spring Lane and told me to take her to Spring Grove Mental Hospital. She told me to take the fastest route possible. I stated, "That will be the beltway, but it will cost you."

The beltway is really out of the way as far as travel is concerned for Baltimore City. The best route to the mental hospital would have been straight through the city.

While driving the lady stated that she was taking her daughter, who was a drug patient, some clothes. When we arrived at the hospital the meter read eighteen dollars. The woman stated, "I'll know better next time. I had no idea that the fare would be this much." Then she asked me to wait for her while she dropped the clothes off to her daughter. When she got back into the cab, she said to take her to the bus stop on Wilkens Avenue. **I started thinking, that in actuality, the cab fare would ordinarily run around eleven to twelve dollars.** It was late at night, and the lady stated that she didn't have enough money to take a cab back to her house. I asked, "How much do you have?" "Twenty five dollars," was the reply. My conscience was getting the best of me, so I asked, "Would you like to make a deal?" "What kind of a deal?"

"I'll tell you what. Let's forget about the meter fare. I'll take you home for twenty two dollars." The twenty two dollars for a round trip was about right. She smiled with gratitude and said, "Thank you. You are a very kind man."

As much as I needed and liked money, I just couldn't bring myself to beat that lady out of her money like that. Plus I would have felt terrible, letting her off to wait for the bus on a lonely corner.

* * *

I was cruising in the 4400 block of Park Heights Avenue when I was hailed by this cute black, twenty-six-year old chick. The time was about 9:20 p.m. She requested that I transport her to Roland Avenue and Northern Parkway. The chick stated that she had to catch the last forty-four bus by 9:30 p.m. I then asked, "Where are you going?"

"I'm going to the Hollander Ridge Apartments," was her reply.

I thought about it for a minute. It had been an extremely slow night. I had about forty-four dollars profit for the evening. My goal was fifty dollars profit if possible. I told the lady that I would transport her home for five dollars. Her reply was, "Really? You are such a sweetheart."

From the time that chick got into the taxi, I knew that she was high, because her speech was slurred. I guess at this point I started feeling her out with conversation. I revealed to the chick that she was going to be my last job for the evening and that I was going to relax by having a *drink or smoke a joint. The woman stated that she had some reefer, and that I was welcome to a joint if I had some papers. I replied that I had some papers in the trunk. I stopped the taxi in the 200 block of West Cold Spring Lane and retrieved the papers from the trunk. The chick told me that this was some good weed and that was the reason for her speech being slightly impaired. I started smoking the joint while I was driving, and I was getting high as a motherfucker. At this point our conversation was getting hot and heavy and we were beginning to have vibrations for one another. She then asked me to stop so that she could get a pack of cigarettes. I was going to stop at the Seven Eleven store on Cold Spring Lane, but she stated that cigarettes were too high in those places. I asked her if she wanted a drink. She revealed that she would like to have one, but her intuition told her no. I could respect where she was coming from, but I drove to the Haven Bar located in the Northwood Shopping Center anyway. En route to the Haven, I passed my apartment complex, so I told her if she didn't like crowds, that I could purchase a bottle and we could have a drink at my place. She thought about it for a while, and I was hoping that her answer would be in the affirmative. "No, I'd better not," she finally replied.*

At the Haven Bar, she exited the taxi to get her cigarettes. The chick ran lightly to the bar; a couple of dudes standing around the outside of the bar made some comments as she passed them.

From the taxi window, I remarked jokingly to the guys, "Hey man, what are you doing trying to hit on my old lady."

When she returned to the taxi, I told her that it would be okay if she sat up front. She replied, "No, I'd better not."

The chick lit a cigarette and rolled another joint. Both of us started taking hits off of the joint. At Hollander Ridge she asked me, "How do you feel?" "Fine, fine ... I feel fine, just really fine. I really am fine."

I realized from talking to the lady that she was really tired. She told me that she had gone to O'Dell's the night before and that she had worked all day. Listening to her, I knew that she was sincere. She stated, "If it wasn't for my being so tired, I would love to hang with you for the evening." "Well, what do you say, why don't you invite me up to your apartment and we can hang together for a little while." "I'm sorry, but I can't. I live with my parents for the time being."

Before departing the taxi, she gave me a five dollar bill, enough weed for a joint, a kiss, and a few words about being such a sweetheart for bringing her all of the way home. ***My reply was that we were all in this world together.*** *I gave her one of my business cards as she departed the taxi. She remarked, "I think you are an interesting cabbie." That really was an interesting twenty to twenty five minute drive across town.*

* * *

I picked up this black male and a child at the intersection of Pratt and Pulaski Streets. He instructed me to circle the block and come back around to pick up his wife in front of McCoy's. Once we were in front of McCoy's, the man exited the vehicle, but he couldn't find his wife. He returned to the vehicle cursing under his breath. He instructed me to drive east on Pratt Street. At the intersection of Pulaski and Pratt Street, he noticed his wife sitting in a Diamond Taxi. As an outsider, the whole mess was really funny. He called to his wife in an angry manner. The little boy seated in the back seat said to his father, "Daddy, please don't argue with mommy and beat her up when we get home ... please daddy."

He told the little boy who appeared to be about four, "Shut the fuck up, and get your ass out of the taxi." After the man paid the fare and departed, I wondered why he had to talk to this child in that manner, and I also wondered how much this child had been exposed to.

* * *

I picked up these two black men at the intersection of Liberty Heights Avenue and Reisterstown Road. They stated that it was terribly cold out there, and that they were damn glad to see an available taxi. Both guys stated that they were cement finishers on bridges being rebuilt around the city. The man seated up front stated that he had been in the joint for seven years. He revealed that at times he had better times in the joint than on the outside. He said, "Man, when I was in the joint, I made big bucks because I worked in the visitor's room. I would charge inmates at least twenty five dollars to get drugs, money and whiskey upstairs in the jail. By the time I was paroled, I had saved up damn near seven grand." The man also revealed that when he was on the work release program, he used to leave the jail at 5:00 a.m. and didn't have to return until 9:00 p.m. At times he said his employer on the outside would cover for him while he visited friends or went to see a girl. He stated, "To survive the last three years in the joint, I had to smoke dope every day."

The man appeared now to be a hard working guy, stating that he had paid his debt to society. He said, "All of that shit is now in the past." He and his friend got out of the taxi in Northwest Baltimore and he stated that he was going to see his parole officer.

* * *

Traveling on Linden Avenue approaching North Avenue, a black male flagged me there and pointed to a dude in a wheel chair. I really didn't want to be bothered with a wheel chair passenger, but in my heart I couldn't turn the dude down. After helping him into the cab, he said that he wanted to go to the Amtrak Station. While making a U-turn at North and Eutaw, he changed his mind and told me to take him to the Trailways Bus Depot. While driving, I started asking myself, **"Where in the world is this man going?"** *He was about twenty three years old, and both of his legs were cut off as far as possible. We didn't talk very much. When approaching the station, I had to ask him, "Where are you heading?" "I am going to New York," the man replied. After retrieving his chair from the trunk, the*

man maneuvered himself into it, and I wheeled him into the station.
After returning to the cab, I rolled passed the station, and I noticed the man talking to someone at the ticket counter. I had a very strong admiration for the man, but in reality, I had to wonder how this man was going to make it being a burden on others until he reached his destination. I wondered how he would fare in New York. I, a man with a healthy body and two legs, am a bit hesitant about venturing to New York City alone. This man has to be one of the most courageous human beings in the world.

* * *

I picked up this young couple at North Avenue and Belair Road who appeared to be in their early twenties. They were well-groomed. They requested to be transported to the Westport section of the city. The man asked his lady, "If I get this job in Boston, will you go with me?"
She replied, "I'll go anywhere with you, as long as you take care of some of my needs."
"I heard that," he replied. The couple talked all of the way to their destination and not once did I hear them complain or talk about anyone in a detrimental or negative way. The lady revealed something to her man, then I heard her say, "You know I want a hell of a lot, and you know that I am willing to work to obtain some of my goals."
After the man paid the fare, I watched them as they walked from the cab, and I said to myself, ***"They really appear genuine and lovable."***
I was hailed at 33rd Street and Greenmount Avenue by these two foreign exchange students. They requested to be transported to North and Calvert. En route, the man seated up front stated, "Life is really funny."
I replied, "I don't know how funny it is, but at times it can be hard."
He then asked, "What do you think about women?" I replied, "At one time I didn't think very much of them

collectively, but at the present time I have one that I love."

He went on to state the American women do not know what real genuine love is, and that they only equate love to a man's pocketbook. He continued to convey that in this country as long as the man's money is right, there is no problem with the relationship. But when the cake becomes short, the relationship turns sour, or the chick starts outside dating.

The foreigner was generalizing about American women but to some degree, through my experiences, he was absolutely right. I've been involved with women from just about every economical status and for the most part they all want to be treated like a lady and want you to spend that cake on them. I do not believe that a relationship can be formed between a man and a woman without the man getting off that cake. I've never been in a bar or a club and a chick sent me a drink, but on occasions, I've done this along with other men sitting in bars looking for conversation or a companion for the evening. In reality, these chicks are out there looking for a little play themselves. As a cab driver, I hear all kinds of shit coming from ladies' mouths relative to how they get over with men. You will hear them say that so and so is good to them; all they are talking about is that he wines and dines them, and occasionally he lays a little cake on them. I would really like to know how they are good to him. Most will probably state that they are good because they give him a little hip. Back to what the foreigner was saying, I'm in agreement with him when he stated that American women do not know the real meaning of love.

I think along his lines that a woman should love you as the individual that you are, regardless of what your predicament might be from time to time. I think that during these inflationary times, love will be stressed more so now since money is at a minimum. Only time will tell!

Hey Cabbie

I picked up this Cuban at the intersection of Sinclair Lane and Moravia Road. He told me to take him to 35th Street and Greenmount Avenue. He told me that he floated over with the rest of the Cubans about six months ago. He appeared clean and eager to get ahead in this country. He revealed that he worked as a parking lot attendant somewhere downtown. He also conveyed that he had a sponsor, and that he was studying English in night school. After talking to this man, I thought to myself **"This man has more ambition than a lot of niggers who are Native Americans."** *The Cuban stated that he really couldn't stand cold weather. I told him that he should purchase some heavier clothing and wear thermal underwear. The man was interesting, and he wanted to learn as much as possible about everything.*

There are several rewards for driving a taxi. The greatest reward of this industry is **MONEY.** That reward is in exchange for a service rendered. This is what we all work for. cold-green-bucks immediately, is just encouragement to go on. The second would be helping others in need. The final reward is dealing with individuals on a one-on-one basis. People are basically good natured and really open up when they are alone. They are as honest with you as you are with them. People are nice as a rule. Some request that you stop prior to their final destination, most likely at a liquor store, and they will ask you if you want something. You learn that circumstances in this society make many act and react the way they do. Some groups of people that have no control in a society must react loudly in order to be heard. In most one-on-one situations, people will tell you everything in a matter of seconds.

The source of a patron's generosity regarding the size of a tip is unknown and unpredictable. For the most part it probably is learned behavior. Then it could be circumstances that contribute to one's happiness during that particular time. Then it could be pay day, check day, or a piece of unearned money received. It could be the mood of an individual at that precise moment. Whatever the reason, all cabbies will welcome any monies in addition to the fare.

I bidded on this call in the vicinity of 39th and Charles Streets. I was dispatched to the 3700 block of Charles

Street. This section of the city is known as Guilford, which is supposed to house the elite WASP of the city. After blowing the horn, this white female about eighteen years old, came out of a house and entered the taxi. She told me to take her to the BWI Airport. I was bubbling with joy because that is about a ten dollar job. **Man you just can't imagine what ten dollars means to a cabbie!**
En route we started talking and she stated that she was going somewhere in Ohio. She continued to convey that this was her first flight. "I'm really very nervous," the young lady stated. "It is only a short flight to Ohio, and before you know it, you will be there," I assured her.
"I know, I know, but I'm scared."
"Well just relax. There are far more automobile accidents than airplane accidents. Just try to be calm. If anything is going to happen, then it is meant to be!"
"Thanks a lot."
"Really, the way airports are set up today, you don't even realize that you are leaving the place. If necessary, have a drink before departure." **I could not figure if this young lady was running away or not. I observed no luggage in her possession.**
At the airport, her fare was eleven dollars, including the charge for the call. After paying her fare, she thanked me for the conversation. She said that my conversation helped to calm her nerves, and to thank me, she gave me a ten dollar tip. I thanked her very much and told her to have a safe flight.

All taxi drivers in this city are individual businessmen to the fullest extent. It costs one dollar annually for a Public Service Badge, and you do not have to be a United States citizen. Have you ever noticed the number of foreigners who operate cabs? They do not know the language very well, and they can't find ninety percent of the streets around town.

In order to survive in this industry, one must have a clear head, and positive thinking is an absolute must. If you get something on your mind or interference that causes delays, you will not make money. A hustler lets nothing get in his way until he has achieved his goal. A professional cabbie knows the city streets, and if he is not aware of a particular location, then he is prepared with street guides or maps, "*Baltimore's Good Times*" **promotional paper** concerning events in the city, and a polite attitude. **Cabbies are "Ambassadors of Goodwill" to the city. If their mannerisms are not intact, this creates an image problem for Baltimore.**

An old man once stated to me, "Son, you get no more out of life than what you put in it." I understood exactly where he was coming from concerning life, and in this industry it is as accurate an axiom as possible. People enjoy a talkative and friendly cabbie. This helps many get through their day. They seem to want to feel relaxed between whatever. This friendly attitude and some congenial conversation can do much to encourage a tip as well as enhance the size of the tip.

If you are a perceptive person, you will not miss much as a cabbie. It will become easy for you to recall places and situations with and regarding your patrons. Driving a cab contributes a lot of exposure to the individual's mind. You see it all, especially regarding people. It gets to a point that after you have heard ten problems, you have heard the problems of the world. But you keep listening, and you must treat each patron and his problem as a unique situation. Most problems are centered on, money, sex, drugs, or power. **It gets to a point that you accept PEOPLE AS PEOPLE, no matter what they have, or do not have in life. Most people's problems are based on similar circumstances. The major difference is who deals with people's problems and how much money you have to deal with your problem.**

The commercialism of holidays can freak you out concerning the retail industry. They are very good planners and they stay in the future relative to that **BUCK.** Christmas Eve, the retail stores will be dressing the mannequins with swimwear or preparing for some other season aways down the road. They also reduce everything Christmas Eve. It makes you think just what is it all about. But this is the only way that business can stay alive - stay ahead of the game. It is no different in this industry. You must stay ahead of the game.

As you cruise the streets in search of that fare, you cannot help but notice the insurmountable number of people who stand around, I guess waiting for something to happen. Many of these people appear so far gone that they could not work, even if someone gave them a job. Man was put here to occupy himself relative to doing something constructive with his life. These street-hanging people are standing on corners, drinking cheap wine and dealing in drugs, waiting for some miracle to come their way. Their lives are just non-productive and they are a threat to everyone, including themselves.

The rich and the poor seem to be on the same level in life. They both seem to have the essentials of life. The rich have it through the power of money, and the poor have governmental agencies relief support programs. Both of these groups can enjoy portions of everyday to a degree. Middle class people do not know what is happening, or which end is up. They are constantly struggling to stay in the middle. Their lifestyles appear to be working and sleeping.

Baltimore is a real prejudiced town and the people make it that way. This is a blue collar industrial town with a lot of underlying subtle ways. It contains a lot of migrants from the South, both blacks and whites. The people are not open-minded, and they are very hostile and over protective of what they perceive to be their little corner of the world. People, especially the middle class, are very possessive of "their turf." The blacks are just as guilty as the whites. It will probably never change.

People, who have class that live around center city, do not display much prejudice. You do not see much prejudice among fags, prostitutes, junkies and people who are incarcerated. But you see plenty of it in these old ethnic neighborhoods. As a cabbie, I actually see people for what they are, no more, no less. What I mean is that the important ones or the majority are no different than me, you or anybody else. They only think they are.

I let this fare out on the St. Paul Street side of the Amtrak Station. As one fare alighted, this fare got in at the same location. He stated that he wanted to go to the main Post Office. For some reason I figured that this dude was a high ranking official in the Post Office. I revealed to this businessman that the dude who just departed the taxi worked for the Post Office in Washington, D.C. I told him that the other guy told me that it runs him about seventy six dollars a month for transportation to and from D.C. I then asked the passenger in the taxi was it worth it.
"You wish you were that lucky."

Hey Cabbie

I revealed to this man that I was once an employee of the United States Post Office and that there was no way in hell that I would want to work for any segment of that place again. He got to talking about the benefits and all that shit.

The man abruptly changed the subject by talking about Baltimore taxis being the highest on the east coast. He stated, "You start off at a dollar, a thirty cents surcharge, plus twenty five cents for a call." "But, there is no surcharge in this city." "You people should be glad that someone called you for transportation, and the company shouldn't charge anything for calling a taxi to a particular location."

I was wrong about this guy being a postal official. *He went inside and checked his postal box. After listening to this man talk, I came to the conclusion that he was one of those people who thought that his shit didn't stink. He was nasty and a know-it-all about everything. He got back into the taxi and told me to drive to Mount Royal and Calvert via Fallsways. At Mount Royal and Calvert, I asked him which corner he wanted to get out on. He then instructed me to drive North on Calvert Street to 34th Street. I hate people who want me to take them someplace but won't give me their destination. All they do is advise you to turn when you approach the street that they want you to turn on. When we approached 34th Street, he advised me to continue on to the alley on the left and make a turn. He then asked me to pull up to the side entrance of the Marylander Apts. I swear that I had no idea where this man's destination was until I got him there. This man must have had bullets for lunch, he was the nastiest bastard that 1'd ever met. I was damn glad when he got the fuck out of my cab.*

* * *

This woman and her teenage son hailed me at the intersection of Gwynns Falls Parkway and Garrison Boulevard. Their destination was Security Mall. En route to the mall, the son pulled out a snack from his coat pocket. His mother intervened by stating, "I know that you are not going to eat that in this cab, and where is your class?"

The lady was absolutely right! Many cab riding Baltimoreans have no class whatsoever. They eat everything in the cab, but when they eat chicken, many throw the bones out of the window. They also leave greasy spots all over the seats, which may soil other fares' clothing. While talking about this incident, I thought of another annoying problem of Baltimore cab riders. Some dudes will holler and make remarks out of the cab window to females that appear attractive to them. It's really no sense saying anything to these types of individuals. All I want to do is to get them to their destination quickly.

* * *

I picked up this black male about fifty-five years old at North Avenue and Chester Street. He stated that he wanted to go to White Avenue and Harford Road in the Hamilton section of the city. He revealed that he was going to help his aunt who had just received an inheritance from her dead sister's estate. I stated that I wasn't aware of the fact that blacks lived in that section of the city. My man stated that he wasn't aware that colored people lived in that neighborhood either until his aunt died. **Older blacks still have a tendency to refer to the American black race as Negroes or colored people.** *This man then had the nerve to tell me that he had a note in his pocket revealing what his business was in that particular neighborhood, if stopped by the police or, if he was approached by some of the residents. I couldn't believe what this man was telling me. Here we are in the latter part of the twentieth century, in supposedly free America, land of opportunity, Charm City USA, freedom state, and this man thinks that he has to have a note in his pocket because he is a black man who must travel in a white neighborhood,* **"Are we second class citizens ... Is this South Africa, or what?"** *This was just so hard to* *believe and hear, but the man was an older black, and I know from experience that he possesses a healthy fear. But I also think, after listening to this individual, **man**, that as a race of people, we have been brainwashed by the majority, which contributes to our stagnation as a group. As an individual, I really don't think that we should fear until or unless there are serious reasons to fear. I know from experience in my years that the future of the unknown isn't certain with anyone or anything.*

The media can do a job on the minds of people. They sensationalize on anything they deem news worthy. Most crime situations appear to mushroom into something much more than what they really are. This contributes to people not coming out of their doors after dark and knowing virtually nothing about their neighborhoods. Practically nobody walks neighborhoods in this city after dark - everybody is "scared." Some of the fears are justified and some are just blown out of proportion by prejudice and ignorance.

In the City of Baltimore, there is no formal training for a cabbie. He is instructed in company policy and issued a vehicle to earn some money. **The average cabbie learns through trial, error and instinct.** In order to make it in this industry, one has to be assertive and aggressive. You also must be very hungry. One learns to persevere quickly.

As a cabbie, you condition yourself to expect almost anything. The frustrations of the industry are almost endless. You see people as themselves with their animalistic displayed behaviors in their quest for survival. We are no different than an ant or bee colony, one leader with millions of followers. I have actually seen Baltimore, or any other large metropolitan city for that matter, for what it is, a CIVILIZED JUNGLE.

A cab driver has to be a tough animal dealing with the street-wise, non-working people. They will definitely try to game you, anyway they can. Nothing in my years can relate to the experiences of the last three years as a cabbie. Not even a BS degree in sociology, eight years of work as a Baltimore City patrolman and vice detective, nor my professional sales experiences combined, come close to life as a cabbie.

Hey Cabbie

This black kid about fourteen years old flagged me in the 2500 block of Greenmount Avenue. He instructed me to take him to the 1600 block of North Bond Street. After telling me where he wanted to go, the boy pulled his baseball glove from under his jacket. I inquired of the child whether he had a game to play or had he played already. He said he had played some other little league team. The 2500 block of Greenmount is a long rough ghetto block. The child valued his glove, and he was concealing it to prevent any of the Greenmount hoppers from taking it away from him. Children of the ghetto have a rough time walking through strange neighborhoods by themselves. The youngster probably learned from a past experience that you are basically out there alone.

It was a typical Friday evening and I was cruising downtown in search of my last fare in order to achieve my goal. I had lost three hours out my twelve hour shift taking care of personal business and was determined to go home with $50.00.

Two black males standing in front of the bar next to Trailways Bus Station flagged and asked how much would it cost to take them to Cedonia. "About $8.00 including night surcharge," I yelled out the window.

They said, "That's not bad and got into the cab." One sat up front. He was about 5 feet 8 inches, about 155 lbs., dark skinned, wearing blue jeans and a dark jacket. The dude who sat in the right rear seat was about 6 feet tall, 175 lbs. wearing a long raincoat and carrying a yellow plastic shopping bag. They were dirty in character, but I've hauled worse. Once seated, the dude up front said, "Take us to Sinclair and Bowleys Lane."

While driving up Howard Street nearing Saratoga, and at the extreme curve of the northeast corner, we noticed this 6 feet 4 inches tall black slender male with shoulder length hair, dressed in black and wearing a three-quarter length cape fastened at the neck. He was shouting from the top of his lungs in no clearly understandable language without an audience or anybody paying any attention. This man really appeared to be in another world. Moments later he pulled this 14 inch gold cross from underneath his cape, held it high over his head at its base and continued to shout **"IT'S OVER."** I had the green light, and as I passed we all turned to our right saying what the fuck was that, and what does he mean "IT'S OVER." I was trying to remember where I had seen this man before. It finally came to me ... he was the man dressed in black whom I picked up on Park Heights Avenue with the wife who looked like the town floozie.

I said to the dudes, **"I can't imagine what's in mental institutions. Baltimore has a lot of crazies on the streets."** I told them I was curious about that individual, and I asked them could I circle the block to get a closer look. "Naw man, we're in a hurry," they said.

"Okay man," then I made the right turn onto Mulberry Street and over the Orleans Street Viaduct. The dudes carried on a normal conversation between themselves while riding. When approaching their destination the one up front said, "Yoe, better still, take us to Eastbury and Sinclair." This request made me become suspicious; I recalled one getting in with a shopping bag and cabbies being held up and/or killed on the parking lots in that general vicinity. It was only 9 p.m., but that still didn't stop me from thinking of them as the enemy. They instructed me to make a left turn at Eastbury. This is a dead-end street after about a half block in, with poorly lit parking lots on both sides where it stops. The dude in the backseat said that his girlfriend lived further back in the court, and he told me to make a left turn into this dark-assed parking lot.

The cab that I was driving was an older model, and the door had to be partially open for the inside dome light to come on. I made a wide swing to the left as to go into the parking lot and came to a complete stop; opened my door to activate the inside light and said, **"FELLOWS THIS IS IT ... I DON'T DO PARKING LOTS!** The fare is $7.50."

The one in the back asked, "Do you have change for $20?" "Yea," I said. I turned around to find out what he was doing because I heard something rattling.

"I'm searching for my wallet; it's at the bottom of the bag." Then he said that he was hungry, and that he was going to get his girlfriend to cook them a steak dinner once they were in the apartment. I turned around again, and this bastard had this single barrel shotgun with the barrel showing trained within 12 inches of my head. He shouted **"HOLD UP, HOLD UP, turn the GODDAMN LIGHT OUT."**

"OH SHIT THIS IS IT," I said to myself.

The filthy bastard up front did a quick search of me saying, "You don't have a gun do you?"

I never said another word. Needed all of my energies to think my way out of this! I couldn't believe this. These people were actually going to kill me, not knowing how much money I had or how long I'd been on the street. I was pissed! **WHAT HAS SOCIETY DONE TO MAN THAT THE POOR HAVE TO ROB THE POOR TO LIVE . . . DRUGS, HIGH INFLATION, AND UNEMPLOYMENT WILL GET US YET!** ***Poor people have been living in fear of each other for years.*** *I felt like saying, "Why do you want to rob a poor hustling slob like me trying to make an honest dollar." It was extremely cold outside. The thought ran through my mind that if I turn the light out I'm dead. After robbing me, they might kill me or tell me to get in the trunk where I would freeze to death. Those thoughts infuriated me. I was cool, didn't panic, and thoughts ran through my mind of what my tug boat Captain fare had told me. "You must be in charge," activate my plan, if ever caught up in this situation. I was thinking like a rat. I'm not going into a hole without figuring a way out. My main concern was to get this visible advertised cab back onto the main thoroughfare. When I made the quick left turn onto the parking lot incline, I'd positioned the front of the cab on an angle facing Sinclair Lane.*

The man kept saying, "...turn the goddamn light out and give me that fucking money."

*I was still in control. All thoughts ran through my head and I've often said when it goes down, **"WE ALL DIE TOGETHER!"** I kept the light on with the door partially open. The cab was already in reverse. Went back about 15 feet, snatched the gear shift in a forward gear and floored the gas pedal of that slow-ass moving cab. I never looked back at the dude holding the shotgun. The man up front didn't know what to expect. He braced himself by holding both hands on the dashboard. He knew that I was going straight through the intersection without stopping. I was looking for a tree on my right going down Eastbury so that I could crash on the right which would force the creep's head up front through the windshield. There were no trees. These were the longest 45-60 seconds in my life. At full speed I hit the curb of Sinclair Lane's median strip, praying that the gun wouldn't go off while blowing out the front right tire. I drove the cab about 75 feet up the middle of the median strip. I can't recall if Sinclair Lane was busy with traffic or not. The cab died because of the blowout.*

I jumped out, left the money bag on the seat and ran to the left. They got out of the cab quickly and ran to the right. There again I feared being shot in the back while running, but I couldn't turn around at that moment. Later I turned around and noticed them as they did me from a distance after feeling safe. They then ran between the end groups of houses located in the middle of the block on the odd side of Sinclair Lane. I ran up the street, crisscrossing my hands over my head and flagged down an oncoming motorist. Told him that I was a cab driver and I had just been involved in an attempted shotgun robbery. I begged him to please let me in and to get me out the area. He told me that the police were across the street on the southwest corner of Sinclair Lane and Moravia Road. Approached the cop, told him that I was a cabbie and was just involved in an attempted shotgun robbery and holdup. We canvassed the vicinity for the suspects in the cop's car. They were hiding well because I don't believe they could have afforded to live in the area.

I asked where was the police helicopter, and he said the winds were too gusty for it to be up.

We returned to the cab. Traffic was almost at a standstill with motorist wondering why the cab was in the median strip with three doors wide open, headlights on and the motor running. They were looking for blood. By this time five police cars and the supervisor were there. My thoughts were that they should have been canvassing the area and/or waiting on the outer perimeter for the suspects. The cab radio was still working and the money bag was intact. I keyed the mic, called the dispatcher and informed him what had happened. Told him that a tow truck was needed. I wanted to look further for the suspects, but the policeman appeared eager to write his report. I had a few moments of silence after the police officer was finished with me, and I took time to **THANK GOD THAT I WAS ALIVE AND NOT HURT.**

I wanted to make fifty bucks. I'd set my goal for the end of the day. Last time I picked up a fare without proper screening I lost valuable time in court. This time I lost time and money; however, I escaped with my life. In this business you never know. The tow truck finally arrived. I found myself talking about the incident for the next two weeks after other cabbies found out what went down. I told my friend what had happened later that night. She started crying and feared for me. The next day, I found myself back at the cab company with my public service badge standing in line waiting to ask the dispatcher for a cab manifest to go back out on the streets. All I could say was that it was the first of the month, and I couldn't afford to stop; I can't think of yesterday's shit - . . . . . .

Life must go on . . . !

Hey Cabbie

ORDER INFORMATION

HEY CABBIE II   Price: $9.99
                         P & H: 3.00
                         Total: $12.99   Qty _____

HEY CABBIE   Price: $11.99
                         P & H: 3.00
                         Total: $14.99   Qty _____

SPECIAL: Buy both books for $25, get free shipping & handling.

Add 6% sales tax to total order. Enclosed is my check or money order in the amount of $ _____ for _____ book(s).

Mail coupon with check or money order to:

Thaddeus Logan
PO Box 23465
Baltimore, MD 21203

www.HeyCabbie.net

Name: _____

Address: _____

City: _____

State/Zip Code: _____

Books make great gifts!
Allow 10-14 business days for delivery.

Made in the USA
Charleston, SC
18 April 2014